D'ye Mind the Day...

John Pepper

Blackstaff Press

Pictures and memories from yesterdays Belfast Telegraph

Published by Blackstaff Press Limited, 16 Donegall Square South, Belfast BT1 5JF.

ISBN 0 85640 111 0

Printed by Belfast Litho Printers Limited.

Acknowledgements
The main source of the photographs in this book is the 'Belfast Telegraph' Picture Library, storage place of pictures either published in the paper or kept for possible future use. Over the years many fine photographers, such as the famous Ulsterman Robert Welch, have contributed work to the paper. A newspaper, of course, draws on many sources and the selection includes some photographs from the archives of the Linen Hall Library and from the Northern Ireland Information Service. Also included are photographs from a collection found by a Belfast housewife, Mrs Mary Todd, in a dusty box in her attic which she sent to the 'Telegraph'. The Linen Hall Library, which has a full set of 'Telegraphs' spanning over a hundred years, is thanked for its assistance with the cuttings included in this book, and special thanks are due to Mr Walter McAuley, the 'Telegraph's' picture librarian.

Every effort has been made to trace the owners of material which may be copyright. In the event of any questions arising over the use of such material, the publishers, while expressing regret for any error unintentionally made, will be pleased to make the necessary corrections in any future edition.

Contents

Introduction	7
The Headline Yesterdays	8
The Working Yesterdays	35
The Town & Country Yesterdays	46
The Stylish Yesterdays	58
The Travelling Yesterdays	68
The Showtime Yesterdays	82
The Sporting Yesterdays	95
Epilogue	108

Introduction

The retired Ulster postman who sighed, 'Ach, sure you miss the old faces you used to shake hands with,' voiced in his own style the irresistible pull of the past.

This collection of photographs and the extracts from yesterday's pages reflect my own vulnerability to the lure of other days and other times. I acknowledge that if someone offered me the choice of a trip to the moon or a ticket to whisk me to the Castle Junction of a century ago, my preference would not be lunar.

Words do not easily capture with the vividness of the camera the quiet placidity of the gaslit era, when there was neither television nor radio, no traffic jams, no motorways, no spin driers, no one-man buses, and the Belfast Telegraph was selling at a halfpenny.

These records were part and parcel of their times. I found them fascinating because they can bring home so strikingly the atmosphere of the bygone streets and the people who strode purposefully through them, the craftsmen typified by the compositor alongside, the landmarks that are no more, the life-style, the fashions that are as ridiculous to us as ours would be to them, the events that made news yesterday and the day before yesterday.

I wouldn't doubt that the people in such photographs as those of Donegall Place at the turn of the century, or those moving at jog-trot speed on a horse tram looked on the pattern of their days much as in the case of the Belfastman who lamented to a friend that if his little girl had been born a week earlier she could have had two goes at the 11-plus.

'Aye, indeed,' came the reply, 'but sure you never think of these things at the time.'

The extensive Belfast Telegraph Picture Library covers every facet of Ulster life and the selections I have made from it are not all-embracing. They could not be. The choice is purely personal. That is the excuse for what may be considered glaring omissions.

The Headline Yesterdays

Tragedy and turbulence, civil strife, disaster on land and sea have made their grim contribution to the headlines down the years. Two World Wars took their heavy toll on the battlefront, and three German air raids brought suffering right to our doorstep. But there were Royal visits to make the headlines, too, the arrival in Ulster of the first American troops to reach Europe during World War II, the celebration of VE Day, and such events as the Festival of Britain.

THE

ROYAL VISIT TO BELFAST.

SECOND DAY'S PROCEEDINGS.

BRILLIANT CEREMONIAL
IN THE
FREE LIBRARY.

THE PRESENTATION OF ADDRESSES.

ENTHUSIASTIC RECEPTION.

LAYING FOUNDATION-STONE OF NEW ALBERT BRIDGE.

THE CEREMONY.

LUNCHEON IN THE TOWN HALL

VISIT TO THE ORMEAU PARK.

PRESENTATION OF COLOURS TO THE BLACK WATCH.

H.R.H. ALBERT VICTOR.

THE NEW ALBERT BRIDGE.

THE ROYAL VISIT.

THE BALL IN THE ULSTER HALL.

A BRILLIANT SPECTACLE.

(BY SCRUMPTIOUS).

The scene which the Ulster Hall presented last night was one of great brilliancy and interest, which has seldom been equalled in Belfast.

Among the ladies' costumes we may select the following for notice :—

Lady Massereene—Pink satin tulle, trimmed with Brussels lace, with loops of velvet and carnations exquisitely arranged in front of the skirt, and looped up at the sides with diamonds

The Hon. Mrs. Walter Forbes wore a magnificent costume of duchesse satin, trimmed with old point lace. The costume was simply made, in long, graceful folds, the general effect being heightened by rubies and elaborate diamond ornaments.

Mrs. Dunville wore an elaborate costume of black lace trimmed with moire and steel, and looped up with diamond stars; white lilac bouquet.

Miss Sayer: White tuille and pink roses.

Mrs. Frederick R. Tobin: white satin, trimmed with silver cord; silver shoes and silver Austrian belt. The dress was fastened at the shoulder with lilies and green grass.

Mrs. Donald Baynes wore a similar costume.

Miss Riddal—Black brocaded satin. trimmed with jet; ornaments, diamonds, bouquet of roses, and lily of the valley.

Mrs. C. C. Connor—Crevette satin, with Brussels lace and flowers.

Down the years Royal visits have been big news stories. The cuttings on these pages are from 'Telegraphs' of May 1889 when Belfast was agog over the visit of Prince Albert Victor. He had come to lay the foundation stone of the new Albert Bridge which replaced the bridge which had collapsed two years earlier. In those days it wasn't possible to reproduce photographs, so illustrations were always drawn, sometimes from a tracing made over the outline of a photograph. A story's importance was then indicated by many-decked small headlines rather than one or two in large type. Then, as now, advertisers joined in on big occasions. The photograph above of Donegall Place was taken some years later when there was another Royal visit. The City Hall was just going up in the background. The statue of Queen Victoria is already on its plinth.

THE BIG BOTTLE

Largest quantity Best quality

2D a Full pint Bottle

CROMAC BREWERY

SPECIAL PORTER

2d

BELFAST

TITANIC LOST

Unparalleled Shipping Calamity

TRAGIC COLLAPSE OF A MAIDEN VOYAGE

REPORTED LOSS OF OVER 1,600 LIVES.

WOMEN AND CHILDREN SAVED.

675 Rescued by Lifeboats.

GRAPHIC DETAILS.

FULL TELEGRAPHIC ACCOUNT.

BY WIRELESS AND CABLE.

An Exchange telegram states—A marconigram [illegible] Cape Race wireless station reports that the Cunard liner Carpathia reached the Titanic's position at daybreak and found only boats and wreckage.

The Titanic foundered about 2.20 a.m. in 41.16 N. 50.4 W.

All the Titanic's boats were accounted for, and about 675 souls were saved, including portion of the crew and passengers, the latter being nearly all women and children.

The Leyland liner Californian is remaining at the scene of the disaster, and is making further search.

The Carpathia is returning to New York with the survivors.

SOME OF THE DROWNED.

An Exchange telegram says—Estimated fifteen hundred perished. Feared John Jacob Astor and Hays, President of Grand Trunk Line, lost.

NEW YORK.—Reported Colonel J. J. Astor and Captain Smith (commander of the liner) among Titanic's drowned.

Marconigram from Cape Race says:—Six hundred and seventy-five known to be saved.

[illegible]

Southampton on Wednesday last, and including the passengers she took in at Cherbourg was 2,358.

A "Times" second edition telegram says:—At two o'clock this morning the White Star Steamship Company, Liverpool, informed our correspondent that they had received a message through the Olympic, which was on her homeward journey, that the Titanic had foundered, and that a large number of the passengers and crew had been saved, and were aboard another vessel. Nothing further could be made known until more news come to hand. Everything was unconfirmed as yet.

SCENES IN NEW YORK.

UNPRECEDENTED CATASTROPHE.

INACCURATE INFORMATION.

NEW YORK, Monday Night.—The latest reports indicate that an unprecedented catastrophe has occurred in the sinking of the Titanic.

Six hundred and seventy-five of the passengers and crew of the vessel are known to have been saved, but 1,300 are not accounted for, although it is hoped that other survivors may be aboard the Virginian and the Parisian, but no reports have been received from those steamers.

INTERESTING PHOTOGRAPHS.

The lifeboats of the ill-fated Titanic were arranged on the double-banked principle, and were operated by the new Welin gear shown in our picture. These patent davits, which permit of the boats being lowered expeditiously, combine a maximum of efficiency and a minimum of complexity and space.

There were a great number of distinguished visitors at the launch of the leviathan, amongst others being the Lord Lieutenant of Ireland and the Countess of Aberdeen, whilst the White Star Company was represented by Mr. J. Bruce Ismay, who also was present at the collision. Our photo shows Mr. Ismay on the extreme left. Others in the picture are Lord and Lady Aberdeen, Lord and Lady Pirrie, and the Lord Mayor of Belfast.

The 'Titanic' captured the headlines when it was launched. It was the pride of the Belfast shipyards — and of the advertisers too. But the joy turned to sorrow when the 'unsinkable' liner went down when it hit an iceberg in the Atlantic in 1912. As the 46,000 ton liner sank the ship's band played 'Nearer My God to Thee'. 1,513 lives were lost. The faded photograph below recalls Ireland's worst rail disaster, which involved an excursion train in 1889. Happy children crowded the carriages as it split in two when steaming uphill on a bright summer Armagh day. There was a death roll of nearly 80.

THE

ARMAGH CATASTROPHE.

THE LATEST PARTICULARS.

THE CONDITION OF THE INJURED.

ANOTHER DEATH THIS MORNING.

ANOTHER BODY FOUND.

TWO MORE DEATHS.

FUNERALS OF THE VICTIMS.

DEEPLY AFFECTING SCENES.

AN ENGINEER'S THEORY.

THE DOOM OF CASEMENT.

DRAMATIC FINAL SCENES.

CHANGED FAITH PRIOR TO EXECUTION.

LAST WORDS ON SCAFFOLD.

CROWD CHEER DEATH BELL.

LONDON, Thursday.

The Central News says—Roger David Casement was executed at Pentonville Prison this morning.

A small crowd gathered at seven o'clock, and remained until the hour appointed for execu-

nesday night, gave definite confirmation to the announcement we published yesterday on the authority of the London "Express" that Casement had been refused a reprieve:—

The sentence of the law passed upon Roger David Casement, found guilty of high treason, will be carried into execution at 9 a.m. to-morrow.

A. S. RUSTON, Under Sheriff of London.

R. KYNASTON METCALFE, Under Sheriff of Middlesex.

O. E. M. DAVIES, Governor, Pentonville Prison.

August 2, 1916.

Ellis, the hangman, a Rochdale hairdresser, arrived at Pentonville Prison on Wednesday night, and at once made his preparations. He examined the trap-door in the execution shed, and tested it thoroughly with a bag the equi-

AMAZING N

WHOLESA

THOUSANDS

THREE-AND-A-HA

MOTORS FR

AN ASTOUN

Political events too, made the headlines yesterday as they do today. The vast throng of people outside Belfast City Hall had gathered on 28 September 1912 to sign the Covenant pledging 'to stand by one another in defending for ourselves and our children our cherished position of equal citizenship in the United Kingdom'. Four years later in April 1914, the Ulster situation was still capturing the headlines with reports of the exploits of the UVF gun runners. Two years later the 'Telegraph' was reporting the execution of Roger Casement, whose attempt to enlist German aid for the cause of Irish nationalism ended in failure and tragedy. The suffragettes, too, were keeping the headline writers, as well as the fire brigade, busy.

T AT LARNE.

JN-RUNNING.

FLES LANDED.

LION CARTRIDGES.

R AND NEAR.

CHIEVEMENT.

CO. ANTRIM MANSION BURNED.

LATEST SUFFRAGIST OUTRAGE.

HOW NOT TO GET VOTES.

ORLANDS REDUCED TO RUINS.

BELONGED TO BISHOP HENRY.

THE USUAL SILLY MESSAGES LEFT.

Orlands—one of the finest old mansions along the County Antrim coast, situated

"WHY WAS NOT CARSON IN THE DOCK BY THE SIDE OF DOROTHY EVANS?"

"COERCION AND BRUTALITY WILL NOT STOP MILITANCY."

"APPLY TO SIR E. CARSON FOR DAMAGES."

"SIR E. CARSON THREATENS TO DESTROY LIFE. WOMEN ONLY DESTROY PROPERTY."

"JUSTICE AND FAIR PLAY FOR WOMEN, OR MILITANCY MUST FORGE AHEAD."

"YOU HAVE BETRAYED IRISH WOMEN. THEREFORE WE WORK WHILE YOU TALK.—TO SIR EDWARD

World War I has begun as men of the 36th (Ulster) Division, mainly made up of members of the UVF, march past Belfast City Hall in the top picture. Below Ulster infantrymen are being reviewed. The conflict overcame all other priorities and a suspensory Act was passed by Parliament delaying the operation of the Home Rule Bill until the war ended. The advertisements for army surplus goods recall the soldiers' kit of the period.

BARGAIN No. P 28

THE
GREATEST BARGAIN
EVER OFFERED.

HEAVY KNITTED CARDIGANS
in Brown only. Soft and Warm.

Sale Price $3/4\frac{1}{2}$ Carriage extra. Per doz. 40/-

BARGAINS Nos. P21 & P22

P21. Grand Bargains in Razors Extra hollow ground. Polished black handles. Medium blades, round or square points. Each 17/6 doz. 1/6 Post free.

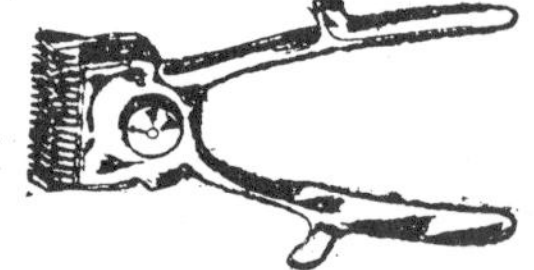

P22 Nickelled finish **Hair Clipping Machine** To cut $\frac{1}{8}$ inch. Sale price Usually 3/6 $3/1\frac{1}{2}$ Post 3d.

BARGAINS Nos. P 35 & P 36

Grand Value in Service Shirts.

P35 Four Clearance Lines.
Army grey, medium, winter weight
Sale Price $1/11\frac{1}{2}$ each. Post 4d.
23/- dozen.

P36 Regulation Army Shirts.
Khaki and grey, heavy and medium weight.
Sale Price $2/7\frac{1}{2}$ each. Post 4d.
30/- dozen.

Left is Private Robert Quigg, one of the Ulster Division VCs. The report below tells of the heroism which earned the awards. Private Quigg went out seven times under heavy shellfire to bring back a wounded comrade each time.

ULSTER V.C.'S.

U.V.F. MEN DECORATED

STORIES OF HEROISM.

CITY PRIVATE'S SELF-SACRIFICE.

A list of Victoria Cross awards issued on Saturday evening contains three names from the Ulster Division, a fact which reflects glory on the province. Two of the recipients have unfortunately not lived to receive the rewards of their valour. The names are:—

No. 14/18278 Pte. WILLIAM FREDERICK M'FADZEAN, late Royal Irish Rifles.

For most conspicuous bravery. While in a concentration trench and opening a box of bombs for distribution prior to an attack, the box slipped down into the trench, which was crowded with men, and two of the safety pins fell out. Private M'Fadzean, instantly realising the danger to his comrades, with heroic courage threw himself on the top of the bombs.

The bombs exploded, blowing him to pieces, but only one other man was injured. He well knew his danger, being himself a bomber, but without a moment's hesitation he gave his life for his comrades.

No. 12/18645 Pte. ROBERT QUIGG, Royal Irish Rifles.

For most conspicuous bravery. He advanced to the assault with his platoon three times. Early next morning, hearing a rumour that his platoon officer was lying out wounded, he went out seven times to look for him under heavy shell and machine gun fire, each time bringing back a wounded man. The last man he dragged in on a waterproof sheet from within a few yards of the enemy's wire.

He was seven hours engaged in this most gallant work, and finally was so exhausted that he had to give it up.

These are the first V.C.'s won by the Rifles since the Indian Mutiny, When Capt. H. E. Jerome, Lieut. and Adjutant H. S. Cochrane, Privates J. Byrne, and J. Pearson were awarded the coveted decoration. Both the old 83rd and 86th Foot, now the 1st and 2nd Battalions of the Rifles, served in the Mutiny campaign.

The faces of these Ulster artillerymen being reviewed by King George V before they left for France seem to express a premonition of the tragedy that was to overwhelm them at the Somme. The news of the battle trickled through slowly at first, but by the end of that week in 1914 the weekly edition of the 'Telegraph' was carrying the Army statement reprinted opposite. The pages of the newspaper were filled with stories of individual bravery, and lists of the dead and missing. Before long, Belfast cinemas were showing a film of the battle to packed audiences.

THE ULSTER DIVISION.

HOW IT WENT INTO ACTION.

LETTERS FROM SOLDIERS.

Rifleman Edward Taylor, formerly of the West Belfast Volunteers, in the course of an interesting letter to his wife, who resides at 34 Hooker Street, Belfast, gives a stirring account of how the Ulster boys went into action. He says—Saturday morning came at last—the 1st of "the mad month"—and then the time came for getting at the enemy. It was a great

RANK AND FILE.

BELFAST.

NORTH DIVISION.

Corporal Scott Bradshaw, West Belfast Volunteers, wounded, is a son of Mr. Thomas Bradshaw, 3 Bradford Street, Old Lodge Road. The corporal, whose injury is to the left hand, was a member of the North Belfast U.V.F., and of Sandy Row Volunteers L.O.L. 1299.

Signaller David Moody, North Belfast Volunteers, wounded, is a son of Mr. Wm. Moody, 16 Movola Street. He is at present at Beaufort War Hospital, Bristol.

BOMBS AND BAYONETS.

SYMMETRY OF BRITISH ADVANCE.

HOW HAPPIEST MAN IN ARMY GUARDED BIG BATCH OF CAPTIVES.

(From Our Correspondent.)

WITH THE BRITISH ARMY IN THE FIELD, September 9.—After a comparative lull of several days, heavy fighting was resumed this afternoon in the region around Ginchy, where Irish troops that have already distinguished themselves in the capture of Guillemont are engaged with characteristic dash and bravery.

AIR STIFF WITH BULLETS.

At 9-30 on Saturday morning a detachment made another attack on Gueudecourt. The air was "stiff" with machine-gun bullets. Nevertheless, they approached within 250 yards of the village, and dug a trench. They pushed out to the left, and tried to extend the line by linking up some shell craters, but the machine-gun fire was too severe, and all were eventually forced to fall back to a new line a little north of Bull's Road, where they

FOR KING AND COUNTRY.

BARR—July 9, 1916, from wounds received in action, Thomas J. Barr, Sergeant Canadian Expeditionary Force, beloved nephew of Thomas Barr, Silverdale, Merryfield Park, Belfast.

BROWNE—Died at No. 2 War Hospital, Reading, on July 11, 1916, from wounds received in action, and was interred in the 14th inst. in Reading Cemetery, Private Samuel L. Browne (Y.C.V.'s), elder son of Mrs. and the late James Browne, 115 Agincourt Avenue, Belfast.

CUNNINGHAM—Died on 7th July, 1916, of wounds received in action, Rifleman Robert Cunningham, Royal Irish Rifles, the dearly-beloved son of Thomas and Rebecca Cunningham, 47 Glenbrook Avenue, Bloomfield.

GRANT—Died of wounds received in action on July 5, 1916, Private William John Grant, Royal Inniskilling Fusiliers, dearly-beloved husband of Maggie Grant, 54 Cable Street.

GRUNDLE—Killed in action on July 1, 1916, Sergt. James Grundle, Royal Inniskilling Fusiliers, fifth son of the late Henry and Mrs. Grundle, Killowen Street, Coleraine.

FINLAY—Killed in action on June 23, 1916, Trooper William Finlay, North Irish Horse, the eldest son of William and Chetta Finlay, 23 Glenallen Street, Belfast.

GRAHAM—Killed in action on the 1st July, 1916, Rifleman Duncan Graham (No. 17759), Royal Irish Rifles (Central Antrim Volunteers), age 23 years, the second and dearly-beloved son of John and Mary Campbell Graham, Cloughfern, Whiteabbey.

HANVEY—Died of wounds received in action on 2nd July, 1916, 9658, Lance-Corporal Herbert Hanvey, Royal Inniskilling Fusiliers, youngest and dearly-beloved son of James Hanvey, 8 Abingdon Street, B[illegible]

NEW RENOWN FOR JULY 1.

THRILLING STORY OF BRAVERY.

CHARGED TO DERRY'S WATCHWORD.

A PROVINCE IN MOURNING.

WELL-KNOWN FAMILIES BEREAVED.

Special Order of the Day by Major-General O. S. W. Nugent, D.S.O., Commanding 36th (Ulster) Division.

The General Officer Commanding the Ulster Division desires that the Division should know that, in his opinion, nothing finer has been done in the War than the attack by the Ulster Division on the 1st July.

The leading of the Company Officers, the discipline and courage shown by all ranks of the Division will stand out in the future history of the War as an example of what good troops, well led, are capable of accomplishing.

None but troops of the best quality could have faced the fire which was brought to bear on them and the losses suffered during the advance.

Nothing could have been finer than the steadiness and discipline shown by every Battalion, not only in forming up outside its own trenches but in advancing under severe enfilading fire.

The advance across the open to the German line was carried out with the steadiness of a parade movement, under a fire both from front and flanks which could only have been faced by troops of the highest quality.

The fact that the objects of the attack on one side were not obtained is no reflection on the Battalions which were entrusted with the task.

They did all that men could do, and in common with every Battalion in the Division showed the most conspicuous courage and devotion.

On the other side, the Division carried out every portion of its allotted task in spite of the heaviest losses.

It captured nearly 600 prisoners and carried its advance triumphantly to the limits of the objectives laid down.

There is nothing in the operations carried out by the Ulster Division on the 1st July that will not be a source of pride to all Ulstermen.

The Division has been highly tried and has emerged from the ordeal with unstained honour, having fulfilled in every particular, the great expectations formed of it.

Tales of individual and collective heroism on the part of Officers and Men come in from every side, too numerous to mention, but all showing that the standard of gallantry and devotion attained is one that may be equalled, but is never likely to be surpassed.

The General Officer Commanding deeply regrets the heavy losses of Officers and Men. He is proud beyond description, as every Officer and Man in the Division may well be, of the magnificent example of sublime courage and discipline which the Ulster Division has given to the Army.

Ulster has every reason to be proud of the men she has given to the service of our country.

Though many of our best men have gone, the spirit which animated them remains in the Division, and will never die.

L. J. COMYN,
Lt.-Col., A.A. and Q.M.G., 36th Division.

3rd July, 1916.

ALL THIS WEEK

OFFICIAL WAR FILM

The Battle of The Somme

FIVE REELS

"If the exhibition of this Picture all over the world does not end War, God help civilisation!"—
Mr. Lloyd George

"THE BATTLE OF THE SOMME" is the greatest moving picture in the world—the greatest that has ever been produced. A great war picture, it is the finest peace picture the world has ever seen; it is worth a thousand Hague conferences. Wherever it is shown it should make an end in the minds of men to the pretensions of pompous princes who have too long claimed the right as the "All Highest" to doom their fellow-creatures to suffering and destruction for the gratification of their mad ambitions. It is impossible to believe that the world will ever forget this picture; its impression will never fade from the memory of this generation. Men who see it will never lightly talk of war again. In this picture the world will obtain some idea of what it costs in human suffering to put down the devil's domination."—*London Evening News.*

ROYAL AVENUE,
Belfast.

Armistice Day in November, 1918, marked the end of the First World War — and politics in Ireland started up again. These pictures capture some of the highlights of the period. Advertisers, naturally, beamed their appeal towards the mood of the times.

Wearing a cap, Eamonn de Valera, later to be President of Eire, leaves Newry police station to be escorted to the train for Dublin in 1924. He had been arrested for defying a Government order forbidding him to enter Northern Ireland.

The morning after a riot in Little George's Street during the 1921 disturbances when the Ulster Parliament came into being. A patrol picks its way along the stone littered roadway scanning windows for snipers.

Many famous country homes suffered during the violence of the Twenties. Here a group of workers at Shane's Castle, Antrim, pose for a picture after fighting a blaze. The man on the left with a saw was clearly prepared for anything.

The parade in the grounds of Stormont as the foundation of the Ulster Parliament buildings was laid in 1928. Four years later the buildings were opened by the Prince of Wales, later King Edward VIII.

TRIUMPH OF HITLER

MADE GERMAN CHANCELLOR

WITH VON PAPEN DEPUTY

STORM TROOPS RECOGNISED

BERLIN, Monday.—Herr Adolf Hitler, leader of the National Socialists, was to-day appointed Chancellor, after a conference which President von Hinderburg had with Herr von Papen, Herr Hugenberg, the leader of the German Nationalists, and Hitler.

Many of the headlines in the 1930s were about unemployment and depression: some were even more ominous. Left is a 'Telegraph' story from January 1933. It appeared on page 11 — the front page carried small ads in those days. Still there was plenty to smile about too. Hatless, but not showing the least sign of strain, Amelia Earhart, the first woman to fly the Atlantic, was given a rapturous welcome when she landed at Culmore, near Londonderry, in 1932. Pilots of both sexes were glamorous figures in those days — the image helped advertisers sell their wares.

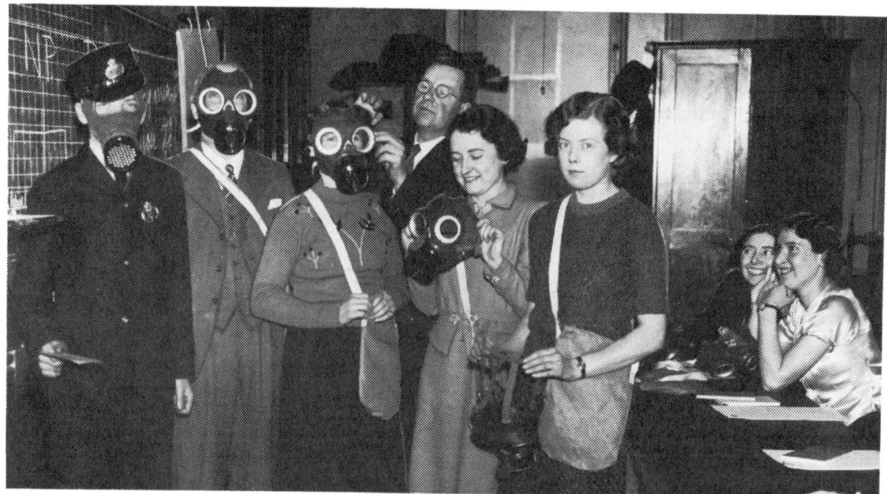

Gas mask drill in Belfast in 1939. Everybody had one — even children, for whom there was a special Mickey Mouse model. Happily they never had to be used.

ATS girls on the march in Ulster. Many thousands were stationed in the Province throughout the war.

And then came the Second World War. It occupied the headlines for five long years and its impact came through in every part of the paper — fashion stories, gardening notes, adverts. The censor was at work, but plenty of news stories and pictures of Ulster at war got by.

IMPORTANT

OVERSEAS FORCES ONLY

THERE is a considerable unsatisfied demand from members of the Overseas Forces for their local newspapers.

The "Belfast Telegraph" is, with the approval of the War Office, in a position to accept a limited number of orders from readers to meet, as far as possible, this demand.

Orders, which should be addressed to this Office, must be written and prepaid, and should not extend for more than three months. Terms for three months, 16s 3d.

The papers will be posted direct from this Office.

"Ireland's Saturday Night" and "Belfast Weekly Telegraph" can also be posted under above conditions. The subscription rates are "Ireland's Saturday Night," 3s 9½d, and "Belfast Weekly Telegraph," 3s 3d.

BLACK-OUT From 8-58 P.M. TILL 5-48 A.M. BELFAST TELEGRAPH, WEDNESDAY, APRIL 16, 1941. 226TH DAY OF WAR'S SECOND YEAR 3

ULSTER BEARS THE FULL BRUNT OF NAZI VICIOUSNESS

The following joint communique was issued by the Ministry of Public Security, Northern Ireland, and the headquarters of the R.A.F., Northern Ireland:

Belfast bore the brunt of the indiscriminate enemy air attacks carried out against Northern Ireland during the night.

Shortly after the alert had been sounded high explosive and incendiary bombs were dropped at random over the city.

A considerable number fell in residential and shopping areas, causing numerous casualties, many of which, it is feared, are fatal.

Other bombs caused damage to industrial and commercial premises.

Whilst the enemy were being met by a spirited defence from the A.A. guns the various A.R.P., A.F.S., and other Civil Defence units were carrying out their duties with courage and devotion under conditions of difficulty and danger.

In other areas in Northern Ireland the intensity of the attack was not so severe, and the casualties were on a correspondingly smaller scale.

These were the headlines in the spring of 1941. On the night of April 16, when the worst of the raids took place, 70,000 people were fed in emergency centres in the city. The scene, left, was Westbourne Street, Newtownards Road.

DIRECT HIT MADE ON SHELTER

Little Family Wiped Out

A number of people were wiped out when a street shelter in which they had taken refuge received a direct hit. A father, mother and their little son were among those lost. An A.R.P. medical officer and a warden are also believed to have been in the shelter at the time.

A woman who was standing in a shelter at the other end of the street told the "Telegraph" that the detonation was terrific, and she thought the whole street of houses had been destroyed. Clouds of dust almost choked her.

A mission hall in the same street was also demolished. All the residents of the houses in the vicinity have been evacuated, and rescue work is proceeding.

THREE ATTACKS IN THIS TOWN.

MAYOR SLIGHTLY INJURED.

SOME PEOPLE KILLED.

Another town was raided by enemy aircraft in the early hours of the morning, when some people were killed and wounded, three of them seriously.

There were three main attacks.

Watchers were thrilled by the spectacle of flares dropped by the raiding planes. These shed a light almost equal to daylight, illuminating the town and also the countryside for miles around.

The situation was well in hand throughout, the A.R.P. personnel, under the direction of the Town Clerk and the

IMAGINATIVE NAZI REPORT.

"GREAT FIRES" AT SHIPYARD

"DIRECT HITS" IN HARBOUR AREA.

To-day's German communique states: On Tuesday night strong bomber formations attacked the important supply docks of Belfast, in Northern Ireland.

The first wave of attackers registered direct hits in the harbour area and in armament works.

Numerous high explosive and incendiary bombs caused great fires in the Harland & Wolff works.

DOCTOR'S HOME WRECKED.

While a doctor was engaged on hospital duty his house was completely wrecked by a bomb.

This dramatic shot shows the enormous bomb crater at the Salisbury Road Depot, off the Antrim Road.

An old-established firm 'crashes'. This is Haslett's in North Street. Arnott's of High Street was another major store destroyed in the blitz.

An impromptu organ solo amid the air raid havoc. This is one of my favourite photographs of war-time Belfast — a superb shot that captures the irrepressible spirit of people at that time.

CUT THIS OUT and keep it as a guide

How to get your new Ration Book

BELFAST CITY AND COUNTY BOROUGH

Surnames Beginning	When to go.	Hours of Attendance
D and E	Monday, 4th June	Between 9-30 a.m. and 5-30 p.m.
F and G	Tuesday, 5th June	
H and I	Wednesday, 6th June	
J, K and L ..	Thursday, 7th June	
M	Friday, 8th June	

WHERE TO GO

BELFAST — EAST.

Y.M.C.A.. Albertbridge Road or McQuiston Memorial Institute, Castlereagh Road

BELFAST — NORTH.

Sinclair Memorial Hall (Duncairn Presbyterian Church). Antrim Road. or North Belfast Mission Hall, Great George's Street

BELFAST — SOUTH.

Crescent Presbyterian Church Hall, University Road, or Smyth Hall, Fountainville Avenue.

BELFAST — CENTRAL.

Ker Memorial Hall, Glengall Street, or Argyle St. Presbyterian Church Hall, Urney Street, Shankill Road.

(Cut this out for reference and watch next Friday's paper for further surname initials)

DESCRIPTIONS OF BELFAST CITY DISTRICTS.

BELFAST EAST—The part of Belfast on the East or County Down side of the River Lagan.

BELFAST NORTH—Duncairn, Clifton and Dock Wards, i.e., the area bounded by Ballysillan Road, Crumlin Road, Clifton Street, North Queen Street, Great George's Street, Corporation Square, the River Lagan and the County Borough Boundary.

BELFAST SOUTH—That part of Belfast to the West or County Antrim Side of the River Lagan and to the South of a line drawn through Falls Road, Grosvenor Road, Howard Street, Donegall Square South, May Street, and through May's Market to the River Lagan.

BELFAST CENTRAL—The remainder of Belfast County Borough.

BELFAST & CASTLEREAGH RURAL DISTRICTS

Hours of Attendance—9-30 a.m. till 1 p.m. and 2 p.m. till 6 p.m.

GLENGORMLEY

Surnames Beginning	When to go	Where to go
A to C	Monday, 4th June	

How to make RATIONS FOR ONE go f-u-r-t-h-e-r

FOOD FACTS

Planning meals is usually easier with several ration books than with just one. But the woman (or man) living alone has this advantage, that she has only her own tastes to consider. The following suggestions show what can be done with a little ingenuity. Women who are alone during the day will also find these hints useful.

What to do when you have to take your meat ration as —

BREAST OF LAMB: Bone and remove surplus fat (rendering the fat down for dripping). Make a savoury stuffing, spread on the meat and roll up. Tie or skewer firmly. This can then be baked, roasted or braised. If it is roasted, cook slowly.

SCRAG END OF LAMB OR NECK OF VEAL: Use it for a stew or casserole with plenty of vegetables (leeks are very good) and some dried beans and peas. Use herbs for flavouring and a dash of vinegar from the pickle bottle.

PORK: Make it into a stew or casserole, using plenty of vegetables and some dried beans or peas. Or braise it on a bed of vegetables and serve pork sausages with it.

Suggestions for easily made main-meal dishes

MIXED GRILL

1 rasher of bacon, 1 sausage, a slice liver sausage, fried potato and peas or beans.

SARDINE AND EGG SCRAMBLE: 1 small knob of fat; ½ small leek, chopped finely; 1½ level tablespoons dried egg, reconstituted; 1 level tablespoon chopped parsley; salt, pepper, and pinch of mustard; 2 teaspoons vinegar; 3 sardines.

Fry leek in fat, add egg, seasoning and parsley, and scramble in usual way. Mash sardines with vinegar, add to egg and mix well.

POINTS CHANGES

For four-week period No. 11 April 29th to May 26th

UP—CANNED LUNCHEON MEATS—6 lb. from 86 to 129; 4 lb. from 57 to 86; 3 lb. from 43 to 64; 2½ lb. from 35 to 52; 1 lb. from 15 to 22; 12 oz. from 11 to 17; any other size or sliced from 16 to 24 points per lb.
CANNED BEANS (in Tomato or Vegetable Sauce). A1 or 16 oz. from 3 to 4; A2 from 3 to 4; A2½ from 3 to 4; 32 oz. from 3 to 4; any other size or loose from 3 to 4 points per lb. (The 8 oz. and A1 cans remain at 2 and 3 points per can respectively.)
BISCUITS—MATZOS from 1 to 2 points per lb.

There will be no change in the value of coupons..
A = 1, B = 2, C = 3, D = 1, E = 2.

DRIED EGGS: The allocation of Dried Eggs is now one packet per ration book every four weeks (as from April 29th); two for holders of green books.

POSITION OF GROCERS.

Many grocers are uncertain whether they should carry on business or not following official instructions regarding the opening of their shops.

The Superintendent of the Belfast Food Office has issued a statement to the effect that grocers during the emergency should keep open under all possible circumstances.

It was important to know where to collect your ration books, while Ministry of Food announcements advised housewives how to spin out the bacon and make fish fritters.

MILLIONTH MEAL OF THE WAR

AT Y.M.C.A. CANTEEN.

The Services' Canteen at the Belfast City Y.M.C.A. to-day served its millionth meal of the war.

Yes, fancy that. A million good square meals for our sailors, soldiers, and airmen in five and a half years of war.

Tea, toast, and baked beans for 6d, or tea toast and two poached

ELEGRAPH, MONDAY, MAY 19, 1941.

GOVERNMENT NOTICE.

EVACUATION

RE-OPENING OF REGISTRATION

PERSONS BELONGING TO THE UNDERMENTIONED CLASSES who wish to be Evacuated from Belfast to the Country AS OPPORTUNITY PRESENTS ITSELF should register:—

(1) Unaccompanied Children of school age.

(2) Mothers accompanied by Children of school age or under.

(3) Expectant Mothers (applicants of this class should bring with them a Medical Certificate to the effect that they are in advanced pregnancy).

(4) Aged and Infirm Persons.

(5) Blind Persons.

DATES FOR REGISTRATION

WEDNESDAY, THURSDAY and FRIDAY, 21st, 22nd and 23rd MAY, 1941,
From 10 a.m. to 1 p.m. and from 2 p.m. to 4 p.m.

OFFICES FOR REGISTRATION

BEECHFIELD PUBLIC ELEMENTARY SCHOOL, Bryson Street.
SEAVIEW PUBLIC ELEMENTARY SCHOOL, off Premier Drive, Shore Road.
HEMSWORTH SQUARE PUBLIC ELEMENTARY SCHOOL, off Agnes St.
LINFIELD SENIOR PUBLIC ELEMENTARY SCHOOL, Blythe Street.

N.B.—Registration provides no guarantee of immediate Evacuation, but is a step which should be taken to secure Evacuation as soon as appropriate accommodation becomes available in the Country.

Ministry of Home Affairs,
Belfast.

THE LITTLE EVACUEES WON'T STARVE

ELABORATE PROVISION

MADE FOR THEIR WELFARE

STATIONS AS RESTAURANTS

PARENTS OF BELFAST SCHOOLCHILDREN NEED HAVE NO FEAR THAT THEIR OFFSPRING WILL SUFFER FROM HUNGER ON THE JOURNEY TO THEIR NEW HOMES IN THE BIG EVACUATION FROM THE CITY.

Plans for their welfare in this direction were made some time ago, and this morning at the three railway stations these were started upon. Seldom, if ever, have the catering branches faced such a huge order.

30,000 CHILDREN TO GO.

To-morrow and Monday 30,000 children are being evacuated, 12,000 each from the Great Northern Railway Station and the L M S Station, and 6,000 from the Belfast and Co. Down Railway Station.

Ten children and one teacher will be allocated to each compartment, and when they take their seats Boy Scout volunteers will hand to each teacher the following ration for each child:

HALF-PINT CARTON OF MILK.
TWO HAM SANDWICHES.
A BUN.
AN APPLE.
TWO STICKS OF BARLEY SUGAR.

AMAZING FIGURES IN BULK

In bulk these supplies reach amazing figures.

The Co-operative Society will deliver at the three railway stations to-morrow morning at half-past six a total of 1,875 gallons of fresh milk.

Messrs. Inglis & Co. supply 3,000 2lb. loaves for sandwich making and 30,000 buns.

Ham amounting to 5,040lbs. has been released by hé Ministry of Food.

A special shipment of Empire apples reached Belfast at the week-end, and 60,000 sticks of barley sugar await their juvenile owners.

The catering arrangements are in the capable hands of Mr. W. Potts Harper, hotels manager, L M S; Mr. D.

Bishop And The Children

Bishop's House, Malone Road, Belfast, July 6, 1940.

Sir,—May I, through your columns, ask the Church of Ireland clergy in their respective areas to see that the postcard given by me through the clergy to each Church of Ireland child is returned to me as soon as possible.

The children may post it themselves (a penny stamp being sufficient), or the clergy may

A group of Belfast evacuee youngsters wait for their journey to safer areas at the GNR station. Many thousands of children — even entire schools — were evacuated. The small boy on the right seems to be in charge of the gas masks in the three square boxes. The little girls at the front are seated on a box containing the baby's protective helmet — a much larger contraption into which most of the infant was inserted.

2 BELFAST TELEGRAPH, TUESDAY, JANUARY 27, 1942.

ENEMY PLANES OVER ULSTER FIRED ON AS AMERICAN ARMY VANGUARD ARRIVES

SPLENDIDLY EQUIPPED DIVISION

Led by Youngest Officer of His Rank

WHEN AMERICAN TROOPS WERE DISEMBARKING AT A NORTHERN IRELAND PORT ON MONDAY THEY HAD NOT LONG TO WAIT FOR CONFIRMATION OF SIR ARCHIBALD SINCLAIR'S WARNING—GIVEN JUST BEFORE THEY STEPPED ASHORE—THAT THEY WERE NOW IN THE COMBAT ZONE.

NORTHERN HOUS
AND U.S. TROOPS
HISTORIC OCCASIO
GOD SPEED VICTORY

Prior to the prorogation of
Northern Ireland Parliament to-
the Prime Minister told the Ho
of Commons:

"Twenty-four years ago
Union Jack and the Stars
Stripes flew side by side at
Northern Ireland port when a m
tary contingent from the Uni
States landed on our shores.

"An event so historic an
significant is worthy of a p
manent record in the annals
this House.

"Those who witnessed as I
the arrival of the troops felt

A great day for Ulster and the Allies — the arrival of American troops in the Province in 1942. These coloured soldiers make a relaxed group on the roadside near Ballymena. Joe Louis, the Brown Bomber, is said to have swung a neat baton in war-time Belfast as a US Army MP. The news item below is from a later period. According to Hollywood's version of events the great General Patton must have won the race.

WHERE THEY ARE TO-DAY

GENERAL Simpson still leads in the race for Berlin, says the British United Press, which gives these distances:—

Simpson to Berlin, 55 miles.

Hodges (near Leipzig), 115 miles.

Patton, 110-125 miles.

Dempsey (beyond Hanover), 130 miles.

Patton to Marshal Koniev (on the Neisse River sector), 110-115 miles.

Patton to the Czechoslovak Frontier, 30-45 miles.

"UTILITY" FUR COATS

THE PURCHASE TAX

COMING REDUCTION.

Captain WATERHOUSE (Parliamentary Secretary, Board of Trade) moved two orders in Parliament the effect of which will be to reduce the purchase tax on certain classes of fur coats from 100 per cent. to $16\frac{2}{3}$ per cent. These coats will be marked "Utility." This would assist those who would like to buy inexpensive fur coats and would help the fur trade.

The children turn out to greet the US troops — and the girls were pleased to see them too. In no time at all they were all chewing gum and forgetting austerity with presents from the PX. Many became GI brides. Many of the rest of us had to be content with duller ways of helping the war effort — such as salvage collecting.

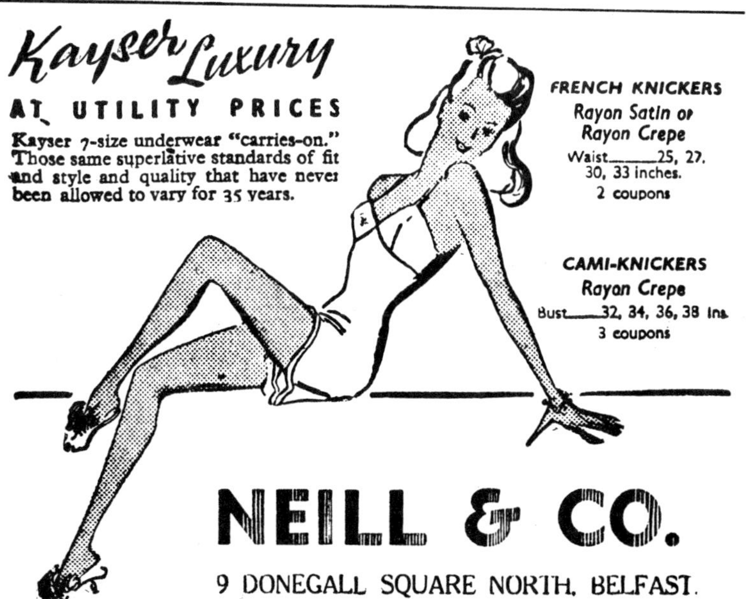

WAR: 36TH WEEK OF SIXTH YEAR BELFAST TELEGRAPH, MONDAY, MAY 7, 1945.

GERMANY SURRENDERS UNCONDITIONALLY

THE ALLIES TO-DAY OFFICIALLY ANNOUNCED THAT GERMANY HAD SURRENDERED UNCONDITIONALLY, SAYS A REUTER'S TELEGRAM FROM RHEIMS.

THE SURRENDER TOOK PLACE AT 2-41 A.M. (FRENCH TIME) AT THE LITTLE RED SCHOOLHOUSE WHICH IS GENERAL EISENHOWER'S HEADQUARTERS.

COLONEL-GENERAL GUSTAV JODL, THE NEW GERMAN ARMY CHIEF OF STAFF, SIGNED FOR GERMANY.

GENERAL BEDELL SMITH, GENERAL EISENHOWER'S CHIEF OF STAFF, SIGNED FOR THE SUPREME ALLIED COMMAND, ACCORDING TO AN ACCOUNT OF THE CEREMONY BROADCAST BY NEW YORK RADIO.

Finally it was all over in a blaze of banner headlines and triumphant cartoons. Stories like that of the redoubtable Fusilier Gillanders lifted everybody's hearts. After two years his eggs must have been fried rock solid, but perhaps some special Victory Heinz sauce pepped them up.

ANNOUNCED DEAD TWO YEARS AGO.

HAS CABLED HOME

"KEEP THE PAN WARM."

Mr. and Mrs. Thomas Gillanders, 69 Ravenhill Road, Belfast, who over two years ago, were officially informed that their youngest son, Fusilier Robert Gillanders, Royal Inniskilling Fusiliers, had been killed in action whilst serving in Burma on January 9, 1943, have received the joyous news that he is alive and well.

Fus. R. Gillanders.

On Thursday last a cable message was received stating:—"Keep pan warm. Home soon — Gillanders," and on Saturday there followed an airgraph letter in Fusilier Gillander's handwriting stating that he had been shot in the head and taken prisoner by the Japanese and that he had been liberated at Rangoon a fortnight ago. He hoped to be home soon.

The War Office report of his death must arose through his pals reporting that they had left him for dead on the field of battle.

Soon now!

after five years with the Services

HEINZ

57

will be home with you again

Always ready to serve

The throng in Donegall Place, Belfast, for the celebration of VE Day in 1945 — a smile on every face. This is pedestrianisation with a vengeance. One local firm was then advertising coverage against 'celebrations damage' at 5/- per £100.

Patches of oil and a few bits of wreck

ONLY 44 KNOWN SU

GRIM RECKONING OF 133 LOST LEAVES ULSTER STUNNED

FULL IMPACT OF THE TRAGEDY of the Princess Victoria struck Northern Ireland to-day when the stark horror of the final moments of the ship's death struggle with raging seas off the Copeland Islands was revealed.

To-day the grim reckoning was made. And the answer—44 survivors out of a total of 177 passengers and crew—left the Province stunned with grief

HE SAW MAJOR SINCLAIR ON RAILS OF SHIP

Man who helped to tie rope round Minister

ONE Belfast survivor, 28-year-old William Copley, a charge hand cleaner with th.. Short Bros. & Harland party, told to-day in his mother-in-law's home at 145 Alliance Avenue, of what must have been the last hours of Ulster's Minister of Finance,

Among the saddest headlines of the post-war period were those of February 1st, 1953, when the 'Princess Victoria' went down on the Larne crossing. Here is an extract from the front page of the 'Telegraph's' special edition with, inset, a shot of the silent crowd that waited for news outside the paper's office.

A report from Orlock Coastguard station this afternoon that another body had been picked up by a lifeboat brought the total of bodies so far recovered to seven.

One hundred and twenty-six people remain unaccounted for, amongst them Major J. Maynard Sinclair, Northern Ireland Minister of Finance, and Sir Walter Smiles, M.P. for North Down in the Imperial Parliament.

AIR, SEA WATCH KEPT

This afternoon, as the 44 survivors—there were no women amongst them—told their stories revealing of the tragic drama of the Princess Victoria, lifeboats, merchant ships and aircraft were searching the area in which she sank.

The wreckage told a pitiful tale. Scores of small rafts to which terrified passengers had attempted to cling in yesterdays raging seas, still floated, their signal lights burning.

A number of them were sighted by the Belfast bound M.V. Ulster Monarch between 10 o'clock and mid-day to-day several miles from where the 2,600-ton Princess Victoria went down.

Aeroplanes circled overhead continuously searching the area for any sign of life, although as the hours passed the chances of any further survivors being picked-up faded into hopelessness.

During the search one of the aircraft dropped a smoke flare and Donaghadee lifeboat was directed to the spot.

RAFT—BUT NO SIGN OF LIFE

From the bridge of the Ulster Monarch a large raft-seat, designed to support 20 people was sighted and the ship turned round.

But that, too, like the other smaller rafts drifting, showed no sign of life.

re only relics of tragic Larne steamer

IVORS OF DISASTER

The Queen wore powder blue

THE Queen to-day was wearing a powder-blue coat with a large fur collar and an off-the-face hat of the same colour surmounted by a feather.

She wore grey sling-back shoes.

Princess Margaret wore a silver-grey silk taffeta coat over a frock of strawberry colour. Her hat, also off-the-face, matched her frock.

Belfast Telegraph

81st Year. Friday, June 1, 1951. Twopence.

Belfast opens its heart to the Royal visitors

SUN SHINES FOR A DAY OF COLOUR

BELFAST opened its heart to-day to the Queen and Princess Margaret at the start of their four-day Festival of Britain visit to Northern Ireland. Brilliant sunshine, cloudless skies, colourful ceremonial and holiday crowds combined to make it one of the happiest of Royal occasions.

Bulletin is issued by King's doctors

bulletin issued by the King's doctors from Buckingham Palace to-day said that the King has "a small area of catarrhal inflammation."

could mean a small area of bronchitis.

bulletin said:—

All the way from the Dufferin Dock to Castlereagh, back to the City Hall and on to Stormont the route was thickly lined.

Radiant as a shade of blue, a carried with it a the full programm

At the present College, Her Majest that he was unable when she said: "Th in a form which boy fore, asking your He holidays."

After a smooth cro Liverpool, H.M.S. Sheffie

To mark the Festival of Britain in 1951, Queen Elizabeth visited Belfast, accompanied by Princess Margaret, who was deputising for King George VI, recovering from flu. The Royal visitors are shown during a tour of the Festival Exhibition at Castlereagh. The Princess was then 20.

The Working Yesterdays

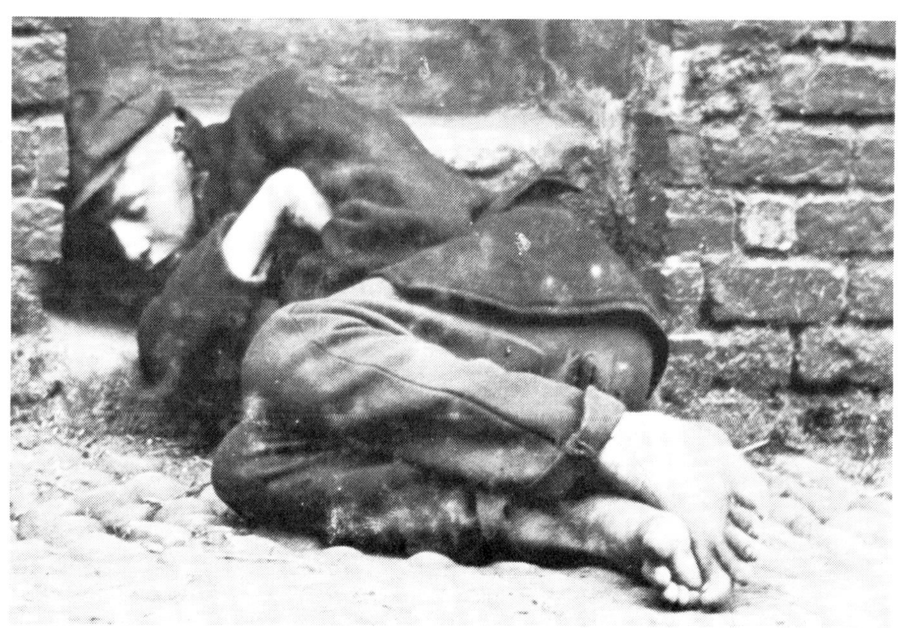

Police court reports in the early days of the Telegraph reflected the period in their own style. The photograph above was taken in the early years of the century by David James Hogg who recorded with his camera the work of a police court missionary. It makes strange reading to have it said a woman charged with vagrancy that 'her antecedents were anything but favourable.' Those were the days when the poor lived in dread of the workhouse.

BELFAST UNION.

LADY SUPERINTENDENT NURSE WANTED.

WANTED, A LADY SUPERINTENDENT NURSE for the BELFAST WORKHOUSE INFIRMARY and FEVER HOSPITAL, which contain about 1,600 beds. Commencing salary £120 per annum, rations, and apartments.

It shall be her duty to take general charge of the nursing of the sick, administration of medicines, distribution of food, and the training of the Nurses, of whom there are about 170, and to enforce discipline in accordance with the Workhouse Regulations

A VAGRANT.

An old woman named Sarah Tumilty was placed in the dock, charged by Sub-Constable Harper, who stated that he found the prisoner begging in High Street that morning. The prisoner, whose antecedents were anything but favourable, was sent to jail for one month.

Mill-doffers, knockers-up and kidney pavers may have little meaning for today's youngsters. They were familiar in yesterday's Belfast, however, when such advertisements as one seeking a young girl as a general maid, 'Knock district, wages £1 monthly', were commonplace.

To the millworkers and the shipyardmen, who often had a six or seven a.m. start, the knocker-up — usually a woman — was as normal in the cobbled streets as the milkman or the postman. Their job was to rouse their customers for work; their usual charge for the service was a shilling or so a week.

A common assessment of meanness in those days was 'Him! He wouldn't even pay for a knocker-up of his own but would be jumping mad if the woman that cost his next-door neighbour good money was half-a-minute late.'

Now even the door knockers themselves are vanishing, although not the wit of the shipyardman. This retains the flavour of the comment credited to the workman who fell from a gantry. When workmates who ran to his help asked him if he was hurt he struggled to his feet saying 'Sure I was comin' down anyway.'

WANTED.

Men Wanted.

Strong Men for Work at Jam Pans. Highest Wages. Apply Immediately —

PRESERVE WORKS,

Ravenhill Avenue.

GIRLS WANTED,

14 YEARS AND UPWARDS.

CONSTANT EMPLOYMENT.

LIGHT CLEAN WORK, GOOD WAGES.

Apply—

TIME OFFICE, LITTLE - DONEGALL STREET,

MARSH & CO., LTD.,

BISCUIT MANUFACTURERS.

COTTON HANDKERCHIEFS.

MANUFACTURERS HAVE VACANCY FOR YOUTH,

Of 16 to 19 Years,

AS ASSISTANT IN PIECE DEPARTMENT.

One with some experience preferred.

Apply, stating full particulars,

To Box 6760, Evening Telegraph Office.

The introduction of universal elementary education in the 1870s meant a much increased audience for the press — and the advertisements it carried. Here are some of the jobs you could have applied for in the teens of this century. And perhaps one of the little boys outside the old Model School found a really exciting job — like becoming one of the brass-helmeted firemen photographed on their horse-drawn engine outside the Chichester Street headquarters.

Sir Robert Baird, one of two brothers who founded the Belfast Telegraph. Alongside is the first advertisement for the paper, announcing that it would contain 'instructive and reliable daily information regarding Public Events'. Sir Robert considered it vital to be at his desk every morning before eight o'clock — and expected an equally early start from his staff. The largest of his array of rubber stamps says ominously 'Complaint'.

THE BELFAST WEEKLY TELEGRAPH,
PRICE ONE PENNY,
THE BEST WEEKLY PAPER,
OF
SATURDAY, 25TH MAY, 1889,
CONTAINS:—

THE PARNELL COMMISSION.
The Evidence for the Defence.

FEARFUL SCENE IN A MENAGERIE.
Another Lion Tamer Mangled.

SHOCKING ATTEMPT AT MURDER AND SUICIDE.

ANOTHER GIGANTIC CONSPIRACY IN RUSSIA.
Wholesale Arrests—Several Regiments Compromised—Suicide of Three Officers.

THE BELFAST ASSURANCE FRAUDS.
Points and Particulars of Prison Life—An Interesting Narrative.

LOCAL AND PROVINCIAL NEWS.

THE ORANGE INSTITUTION.

Ulster Orangeman's Letter.

"THE MYSTERY OF A MILLIONAIRE'S GRAVE;"
Also, the Second of a Series of Complete Stories, entitled—
"THE YELLOW DRAWING-ROOM."
Our New Thrilling Story:
"DESMOND JOYCE, THE GALWAYMAN"
(A Belfast Story of To-day);
And our Continued Story:
"THE EXPERIENCE OF AN INSURANCE OFFICE."

NEW
DAILY HALFPENNY PAPER.

Will be Published on Thursday, September 1, 1870,
THE FIRST NUMBER OF
The Belfast Evening Telegraph.

TAKING into consideration the Progressive Intellectual Improvement of the masses of the People, and the desirability of supplying them, through the medium of

A CHEAP PRESS,

With instructive and reliable daily information regarding Public Events, we have determined on publishing

AN EVENING PAPER,
AT ONE HALFPENNY,

Giving an amount of the LATEST NEWS which no Newspaper issued in the morning can possibly present.

The Advantages of the "EVENING TELEGRAPH" may be summarised thus: It will contain—

The General Intelligence of the Day up to the hour of publication, at THREE o'clock.
Parliamentary Reports, while the Houses are sitting.
Important Town Meetings.
Police, Recorder's, and Quarter Sessions Courts Reports.
Shipping News.
Sporting Notes.
The Market and Stock Reports of the Day throughout the Three Kingdoms, supplied by Telegraph—*thereby anticipating, by nearly twenty-four hours, the Belfast Papers of the following morning.*

The 'Telegraph' vanman's bowler hat and the barefooted boys provide their own contrast in this picture taken at Shaftesbury Square in the days when it was the newsboys' shrill cry which broadcast the big news.

FOR SORE TIRED FEET, CORNS AND ALL FOOT TROUBLES.

WHAT SOLDIERS DO WHEN FEET ACHE, BURN, SMART AND PERSPIRE.

Many readers of the "Belfast Weekly Telegraph" may be interested to know how I permanently cured the extremely painful foot troubles resulting from my first few days of route marching. After numerous powders and ointments had only increased the torture I consulted my medical man, and he explained that corns, callouses, bunions and blisters are simply indications of injured tissues, but that there is really no need of enduring any form of footmisery a single moment. They can all

BURNING, SMARTING & ITCHING FROM CONGESTION AND BAD CIRCULATION
WATER BLISTERS
HIGH HEEL PAINS
INFLAMED BUNIONS
SOFT CORNS, HARD & DEEP CORNS, FLAT CORNS & FISSURES OR RAW PLACES BETWEEN TOES
RHEUMATISM GOUT AND SWOLLEN JOINTS
OFFENSIVE PERSPIRATION AND BAD ODOURS
THICK, DEEP AND PAINFUL CALLOUSES
ACHING ARCH AND SHARP PAINS FROM SHOE PRESSURE ON SENSITIVE NERVES

SORE FEET, TIRED FEET, ANY KIND OF BAD FEET

be instantly relieved and permanently cured by simply resting the feet for about ten minutes in a warm foot bath containing a tablespoonful of ordinary Reudel Bath Salt-

Among the most regular newspaper advertisers in years gone by were the manufacturers of a bewildering variety of remedies for sore feet. Can you wonder, when so many people had to stand at work? Top left are women at work in Gallaher's tobacco factory at the turn of the century, and bottom left, office workers at the Ropeworks in 1899. Women's Lib enthusiasts seem already to be in evidence. They're the ones sitting down.

Despite the rapid industrial expansion in the 19th and early 20th centuries, country crafts still lingered on, as these two photographs from 1914 show. Mrs Annie Collins of Waringstown twists yarn to make harness outside her half door (top left). She was said to be the last of the loom harness makers. The picture below is also from Waringstown, one of Ulster's best-known linen centres, and shows damask napkins being woven on a handloom. Life was probably hard for these two women, but at least they had work. Others were not so fortunate, as is shown by the cutting below from the 1930s.

DINNERS AT PENNY EACH

APPETISING FARE FOR DERRY NEEDY.

200-GALLON BOILER FOR STEW

DETAILS OF COMMENDABLE SCHEME.

Meat	84	lbs.
Potatoes	112	,,
Lentils	70	,,
Mixed Vegetables	50	,,
Onions	21	,,
Sago	30	,,
Salt	2¼	,,
Pepper	½	,,

Although at first glance it might so appear, the above is not the menu for a hungry giant's dinner.

These are details of the quantities of the appetising ingredients that form the recipe for the first of the penny dinners to be served to the needy poor of Derry when the kitchen, organised under the Mayor's Fund opens on Tuesday.

FOOD FOR 1,100 PEOPLE.

At the entrance to the premises there is an office where tickets may be obtained. Single tickets will cost 1d each, while a book of 50 may be procured for 4s 2d.

FARMING IN CANADA

Limited number of boys wanted, aged 15 to 18, for farm training, board and room on specially selected farms, under a definite agreement and fair rate of wages according to age and experience. Free Passage. At 21 boys have opportunity to qualify for a loan towards buying their own farm.

The firm of Cameron is still trading in Ballymena under the same name. Whether your interest was in shipping or cycling you were given a warm welcome. Cameron's must have done a brisk trade during the years when emigration was at its highest. The notice in the window says the fare to Africa by P & O Line was £21 and to Australia £37. At those prices, it's a wonder anyone's left in the old country.

CANADA, AUSTRALIA AND U.S.A.—Passages booked by all lines to all parts. Lowest rates. Salvation Army has weekly conducted parties to Canada. Assisted passages for suitable Men and Women and Families. Domestic Servants wanted. Farm Work guaranteed on arrival.—Full particulars from Commissioner Lamb, 170a, London Road, Liverpool, or 222 Albertbridge Road Belfast.

Canadian Pacific.

CHEAPEST and most CONVENIENT

WAY TO

CANADA

Fortnightly Sailings resumed

from BELFAST DIRECT

APPLY TO

CANADIAN PACIFIC RAILWAY

41 & 43 Victoria St. or Local Agents,

Improved freehold farms in the land of golden opportunities, for what British farmers pay in rent. A week from Liverpool.

25 million acres virgin soil 2/- per acre.

Dairying, cattle raising, fruit growing, gardening. Unlimited market. Grand climate. Thousands of acres in peaches. Ideal social and educational conditions. Government guarantees farm hands and domestics situations. Good wages. Marvellous natural resources await investors.

Write—R. REID, Ontario Government Agent, 163, Strand, London.

This photograph of keel plate No 1,500 on No 17 slip at Queen's Island records a unique glimpse of the birth of a liner. Heavy industry has played a great part in the story of Ulster at work, but all too often — especially in the Thirties — industrial strife and economic recession brought major setbacks and hardship for working people.

BELFAST QUAY SCENES

200 DOCKERS ON STRIKE

ATTACK MADE ON LORRIES

VOLLEYS OF MISSILES

Exciting scenes were witnessed in Corporation Street, Belfast, this morning, when four Great Northern Railway lorries, returning from the deep-water docks with grain, were stoned.

Missiles picked up from a side street were hurled at the vehicles, and the windscreens and side windows of the canopies were smashed.

George Magee and Robert Downey, the drivers of the leading lorries, were struck with stones, and the former had to be treated in the Royal Victoria Hospital.

A BLANK QUARTER.

NO LAUNCHES FROM BELFAST YARDS.

THREE NOTABLE SHIPS.

THE CLYDE'S EMPTY BERTHS.

There was not a single launch in Belfast in January, February, or March, a most unusual state of affairs, and one that tells eloquently of the slump that has set in in the shipbuilding industry. To find a parellel for a blank quarter one has to go back very many years.

The total number of vessels on the stocks is six—three at Harland & Wolff's and three at Workman, Clark's, but fortunately they are, with one exception vessels of very substantial dimensions.

ULSTER'S LINEN INDUSTRY.

The linen trade in the North of Ireland has, in common with most other trades, suffered severely from the present depression, but we should beware of the tendency to give way to exaggerated feelings of despondency as to its future. There are some people who seem to experience a feeling of gloomy satisfaction in repeating that the linen industry is "down and out".

The day's big story is 'Family wiped out at a birthday party' when this picture was taken of the Telegraph subs' desk. Second right is Tom Moles, then editor, who became a member of the first Northern Ireland Parliament. The lady on the left is his secretary, temporarily occupying the chief sub-editor's seat. The news stories of the time echo the way in which the news columns covered all aspects of human life.

STRANGLED HERSELF WITH RIBBON.

TRAGEDY AT WARRENPOINT.

INQUEST ON DUNDALK WOMAN.

A tragic discovery was reported to the Warrenpoint police on Friday, a woman of independent means named Miss Edith T. Coulter, of Dundalk, being found dead in bed at her lodgings, 27, Seaview, Warrenpoint, under circumstances pointing to strangulation.

Dr. Glenny, who was immediately summoned, said that the deceased had evidently been dead for seven or eight hours. She was in her night attire, and everything in the room was normal. There was, however, a broad silk ribbon twisted round the deceased's neck and knotted. Deceased's hands were in a raised position, as if clasping the ends of the ribbon. In his opinion death was due to asphyxia from strangulation.

BISHOP DENOUNCES MIXED BATHING.

"BEAUTY CONTESTS AN EVIL."

GALWAY BAN PRAISED.

"The evils of mixed bathing and beauty competitions" were referred to by Dr. O'Doherty, Bishop of Galway, speaking in Galway on Sunday.

"Attempts have been made—thank God, unsuccessfully—to introduce another evil into this parish, and into this city—the evil of mixed bathing," he said "I spoke about it last year, and, thank God, my words were heeded, but you know that there are people who are continually trying to introduce that evil.

"You know what such people will say, in a 'broadminded' way—that the thing is done elsewhere, and, therefore, Galway should not lag behind. It is done elsewhere, and you might have seen in yesterday's paper that the Pope himself has denounced the evil.

"As I said, last year, no manly man wants mixed bathing—bathing in the company of women; no modest woman wants mixed bathing.

NURSE HIT ON HEAD WITH SPANNER.

ASSAILANT ON BICYCLE.

POLICE SEARCH FOR MAN.

Evesham police are looking for a young man who attacked a nurse at one of the loneliest spots in the town on Thursday night.

The nurse, Miss Postle, who is employed by Mr. J. E. Rudge, at the Abbey Manor, was returning from the cinema, at 10 p.m., when the man struck her on the head with a heavy, blunt instrument, like a spanner, and rode away on his cycle.

As Miss Postle fell to the ground she was struck a second time on the back of the head. Her cries were heard by the head gardener, at the Manor, and he found her in a state of collapse.

No attempt had been made to rob Miss Postle, and the police have been unable to discover a motive for the attack.

The man is described as between 27 and 30 years of age, tall and broad with dark hair and a fresh complexion, and wearing a check cap and a light dust coat.

THRILL IN CHURCH. BELFAST SERVICE STOPPED.

SHOCK FOR CONGREGATION.

PULPIT ENVELOPED IN SMOKE.

When the morning service was in progress in the Macrory Memorial Presbyterian Church, Duncairn Gardens, Belfast, on Sunday smoke began to rise in dense volumes around the pulpit and choir stalls, creating considerable alarm amongst the worshippers.

A picture of a 'Telegraph' office party in the early Twenties highlights the changing face of women at work. Few advertisers today would aim at 'the nobility and gentry of Ulster' as does the superior Mr Carlisle. In contrast are the doffers making aeroplane cloth for the RAF in Ewart's Mill, Crumlin Road, in 1943, in a photograph which had to be cleared for publication by the war-time censor. Was one of them 'Edith', who lost her gold watch on VE-Night?

TO THE NOBILITY AND GENTRY OF ULSTER.

THE Subscriber is prepared to execute all orders in the House Painting and Decorative trade with carefulness and despatch, combined with moderate charges.

Estimates furnished, and competent workmen sent to the country.

DAVID CARLISLE,

PAINTER AND DECORATOR.

28 CORPORATION STREET, BELFAST

LOST AND FOUND.

LOST, VE-Night, Lady's Gold Wristlet Watch, Edith engraved on back.—Box 7318a.

LOST, Friday, Ormeau Road, Young Black Dog, called Pete; reward.—50 North Parade.

LOST, Sunday, vicinity of City Hall, small Black Purse containing notes and bus ticket; reward.—Box 9336a.

LOST, large Bird-shaped Pin, district May's Market, Albert Bridge, 13th inst.; police notified; reward.—200 Cregagh Road.

LOST Saturday evening Brown Purse (Tramore) with notes and coupons. Finder please return to 232 Tate's Ave. Reward.

The astonishing picture on the left sums up the changing patterns of work that this century has witnessed — on the right something that has changed little since time immemorial; on the left an example of modern man's vast technological skills. The post war years saw many new industries come to the Province. And modern life brought a demand for the highly skilled — though the annual salary of a university graduate in the late Fifties would hardly keep his present day counterpart in cigarettes, after-shave and bright shirts for more than a couple of months.

-FAST TELEGRAPH, FRIDAY, MARCH 16, 1945.

Courtaulds to Open Factory Near Belfast: Site of 270 Acres: 2,000 Employes

SITUATIONS VACANT

The Queen's University of Belfast

LABORATORY ASSISTANT

Applications are invited for the post of Junior Technician in the Department of Biochemistry.

The wage scale rises from £182 at age 16 to £377 at age 23, with prospect of promotion at age 21 on passing the Ordinary National Certificate in Chemistry.

DOWN COUNTY WELFARE COMMITTEE

WELFARE VISITOR

APPLICATIONS are invited for a Welfare Visitor in County Down. Qualifications: Applicants must:—

(a) Possess a diploma or certificate from a recognised University in Social Science, or in Social Studies, or its equivalent; or be a graduate of a recognised University and have passed in Economics or Sociology in the Final Examination; or

(b) Possess the Home Teaching Certificate of the College of Teachers of the Blind.

Salary for (a) £445 17s 6d x £19 9s 6d (2) x £18 9s 0d (4)—£558 12s

PUBLIC BOARD NOTICES

VACANCIES FOR HONOURS GRADUATES

(a) METEOROLOGICAL OFFICERS (5) in the IRISH METEOROLOGICAL SERVICE. Salary scales: Man—£570 to £862 after 3 years and then to £1,220; Woman—£570 to £785 after 3 years and then to £1,018. Higher entry on these scales up to £987 (man) and £877 (woman) for satisfactory experience in another meteorological service. Maximum Age Limit: 36 years. Essential: (i) First or Second Class Honours Degree (or equivalent) in Physics or Mathematical Physics or Mathematics or Engineering, or (ii) Degree (or equivalent) in Meteorology.

(b) STATISTICIAN in the CENTRAL STATISTICS OFFICE, DUBLIN. Salary Scales: Women and unmarried men: £589 to £926 after 8 years and then to £1,220; Married men: £589 to £1,060 after 8 years and then to £1,414. Maximum Age Limit: 30 years. Essential: (i) First or Second Class Honours Degree (or equivalent) in Mathematics or Mathematical Physics or Mathematical Statistics; or (ii) First or Second Class Honours Degree (or equivalent) and adequate experience in practical statistical work.

Application forms and further particulars from Secretary, Civil Service Commission, 45 Upper O'Connell Street, Dublin.

The Town & Country Yesterdays

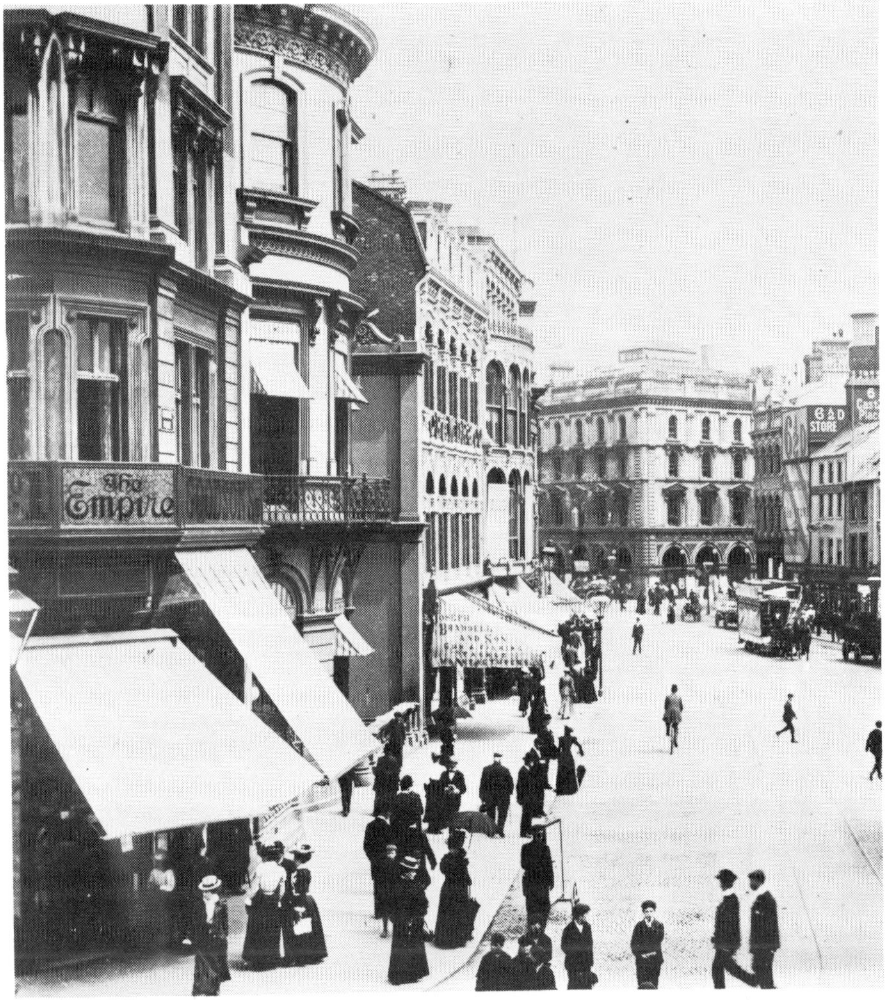
The Empire

A familiar name in this turn of the century shot of Castle Junction is Joseph Braddell and Son, now of North Street. The 6½d Store must have attracted many patrons. Those were the days when 6½d — less than 3p — could buy a lot of merchandise and still leave you with enough change for your tram fare home.

Sandy Row and Fintona, Castle Junction and Rostrevor, reflect in their own way the passage of time. If you ask the way it is the countryman rather than townsman who is still liable to tell you 'Keep right on till you come to a gable whitewashed blue.' While the crossroads may have survived many of the changes of time Belfast's city centre and the heart of Ballymena alike would be unrecognisable now to the good citizens of yesterday.

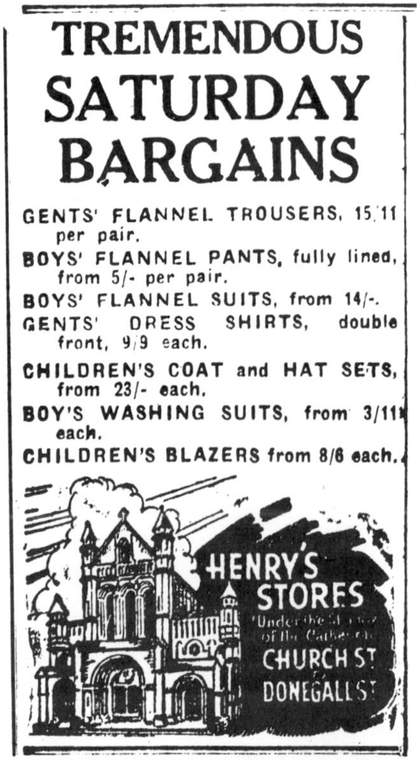
TREMENDOUS
SATURDAY
BARGAINS
GENTS' FLANNEL TROUSERS, 15/11 per pair.
BOYS' FLANNEL PANTS, fully lined, from 5/- per pair.
BOYS' FLANNEL SUITS, from 14/-.
GENTS' DRESS SHIRTS, double front, 9/9 each.
CHILDREN'S COAT and HAT SETS, from 23/- each.
BOY'S WASHING SUITS, from 3/11 each.
CHILDREN'S BLAZERS from 8/6 each.
HENRY'S STORES
CHURCH ST
DONEGALL ST

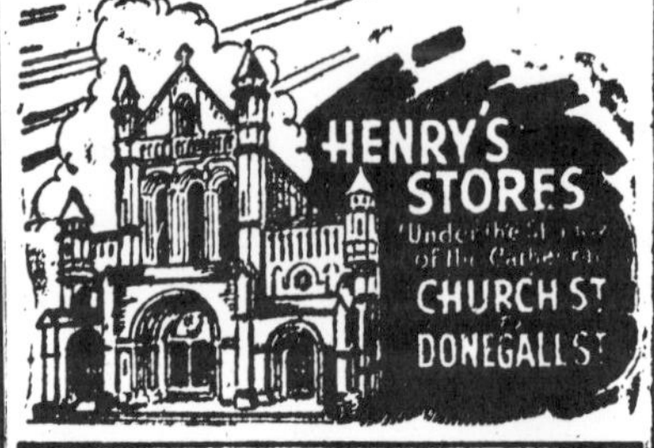

The driver of a low-backed car stops for a chat with a local wiseacre in Rostrevor around the 1890s. What can they have been discussing? The ever-worsening problem of where to park? Or is one saying to the other, 'It's that quiet you could hear the bees belchin'.'

Campbell's tea rooms, opposite the White Linen Hall, as they looked in the 1880s, when Robinson and Cleaver's was newly built and before the City Hall was erected. It was long a haunt of the city's writers, actors and artists.

CELEBRATED SARSAPARILLA.

CANTRELL & COCHRANE'S

AROMATIC GINGER ALE

So celebrated in America, and sold all over the World.

CANTRELL & COCHRANE'S

SUPERIOR LEMONADE,

AND ALL OTHER AERATED WATERS.

BELFAST AND DUBLIN.

Market day in Warrenpoint in 1900 when people went bargain hunting in horse and carriage, pony and cart, or jaunting car. The Paris House has its own special display for the occasion but there is a strangely Wild West air about the entire scene.

TO Let, Shop with Dwelling, Sandy Row; £3 monthly and taxes; in splendid order; kitchenette, electric; price fittings £40.—Garrett, 20 May Street.

TO Let, small Modern Offices, 64 Great Victoria Street (almost facing G.N.R.). 4s 6d and 5s weekly; free electric for lighting.—Garrett, 20 May Street.

TO Let, 27 Denorrton Park, Detached Villa, 2 and 3, &c., electric, garden, garage; rent £55 free.—Garrett, 20 May Street.

FOR Sale, with possession, House, Ogilvie Street, Woodstock Road; contains parlour, kitchen, scullery, 2 bedrooms, bath (h. & c.); g.r. £3, p.l.v. £13; price £225.—Garrett, 20 May Street.

TO Let, 8 Lavens Drive, Ballysillan, small Semi-Villa, kitchenette, scullery, 3 bedrooms, garden; 12s 6d weekly.—Garrett, 20 May Street.

TO Let, nice Office, in good order, second landing, 48 Upper Queen Street; £16 free; very central for agents.—Garrett, 20 May Street.

TO Let, 19 Perth Street, parlour, kitchen, scullery, 4 bedrooms; 13s 1d weekly.—Garrett, 20 May Street.

OFFICES to Let, Marsh's Buildings, Donegall Street, cheap.—Garrett, 20 May Street.

12/6 Weekly.—Holywood: To Let, New Semi-Villa, sitting-room, kitchenette, scullery,

TRILLICK Street (43), Albertbridge Road—New Kitchenette House to Let, 3 bedrooms, rent 10s 6d weekly.—F. J. Lavery & Co., 75 High Street.

BRANIEL Road, Gilnahirk—Choice New Semi-detached Villa to Let, 2 reception, 3 bedrooms, bath, large garden, electric light, rent £52 free.—F. J. Lavery & Co., F.A.I., House and Estate Agents, 75 High St.

SHORE Road (119)—Superior Terrace House to Let, 1 reception, 4 bedrooms, bath, rent £3 15s monthly free.—F. J. Lavery & Co., F.A.I., 75 High Street

CASTLEREAGH Parade (9)—Desirable Kitchenette House to Let, 3 bedrooms, electric light, rent 11s weekly.—F. J. Lavery & Co., F.A.I., House and Estate Agents, 75 High Street.

CREGAGH Street (222)—Attractive new Terrace House to Let, 2 reception, 3 bedrooms, bath, electric light, rent 15s weekly.—F. J. Lavery & Co., 75 High Street.

BELMONT Church Road (35)—Choice Semi-detached Villa to Let, 2 reception, 3 bedrooms, bath, garden, electric light, rent £4 11s 8d monthly free.—F. J. Lavery & Co., F.A.I. Property Brokers, 75 High Street.

PARKGATE Avenue (149) Sydenham.—Desirable New Terrace House to Let; 1 reception, kitchenette, 2 bedrooms, bath, garden; rent £3 monthly free.—F. J. Lavery & Co., F.A.I., 75 High Street.

Sandy Row as it looked in 1910, unexpectedly like it is today. It is doubtful, however, if the words once used of it could still be applied: 'Sandy Row, where they keep no Sunday, and every day's like an Easter Monday.' The property advertisements are from 1936.

The perfect spot from which to see the countryside — the top deck of the Fintona horse train. Horses are no longer shod at the Forge in Antrim, shown left.

Water keeps intruding in the records of Ulster yesterday. Once it was sold in the street by donkey cart, pictured top left. The drinking fountain in Victoria Square no longer caters for city thirsts. In the picture on the left it's a case of all hands to the pump in Ballyclare as the draw-wheel of an old well is moved.

Compared to the little donkey cart opposite, this scene at Wellington Street, Ballymena, shows the Rolls Royce version of water distribution. Naturally pure springs in the Belfast area got the Province's soft drinks industry off to a good start, and still provide such companies with their basic raw material today. Spring water was also an important aid to public health in the days when diseases such as typhus were rife.

Latest Boat Coaches

from 72/6.

200 Prams in Stock from 39/6; also Tan-Sads from 9/6; Cots & Invalid Furniture.

Carriage Paid Ulster. Catalogues. Free.

FREDK. THOMAS

116 ROYAL AVENUE,

Phone 3256. BELFAST.

Cavehill Road, Belfast, showing the cottages which once marked the place where houses ended. Now it is completely built up. The pram in the picture doesn't quite compare with the 'boat coaches' once advertised, prices 'from 72s 6d'.

While Belfast's High Street was always popular with shoppers it once had a cinema — the Panopticon, the sign of which can be seen on the left. Mill Street, Ballymena, had not really been designated a pedestrian precinct when these two ladies stopped for a chat on the roadway. Perhaps the woman on the right is telling her friend, 'That wee lad of mine has my heart scalded. All he does is run the streets in them cut aff trousers.' Or perhaps corn-pinching boots, like those below, were the subject of the conversation.

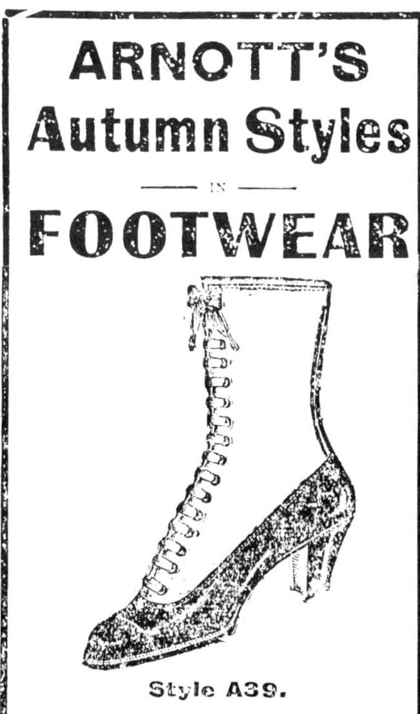

Pop art is strikingly on display in this picture of Bonugli's, still remembered in Larne for its ice-cream. There's a touch of class, too, about the old advertisement below.

IRISH EGGS

These are a little easier now in price. We are offering

Good Medium Sized,

2/2 PER DOZ.

NEW LAID IRISH.

ENFIELD DAIRY CO.

Belfast's old butter market, no longer in existence, is as much part of the distant past as the eggs at 2s 2d a dozen and the boiled lobsters for 6d featured in advertisements of yesterday.

Big plump rabbits from two lbs. up, for 1/4 and 1/6, at Rangecroft Ltd., the Corn Market fishmongers. Boiled lobsters from 6d.

The Stylish Yesterdays

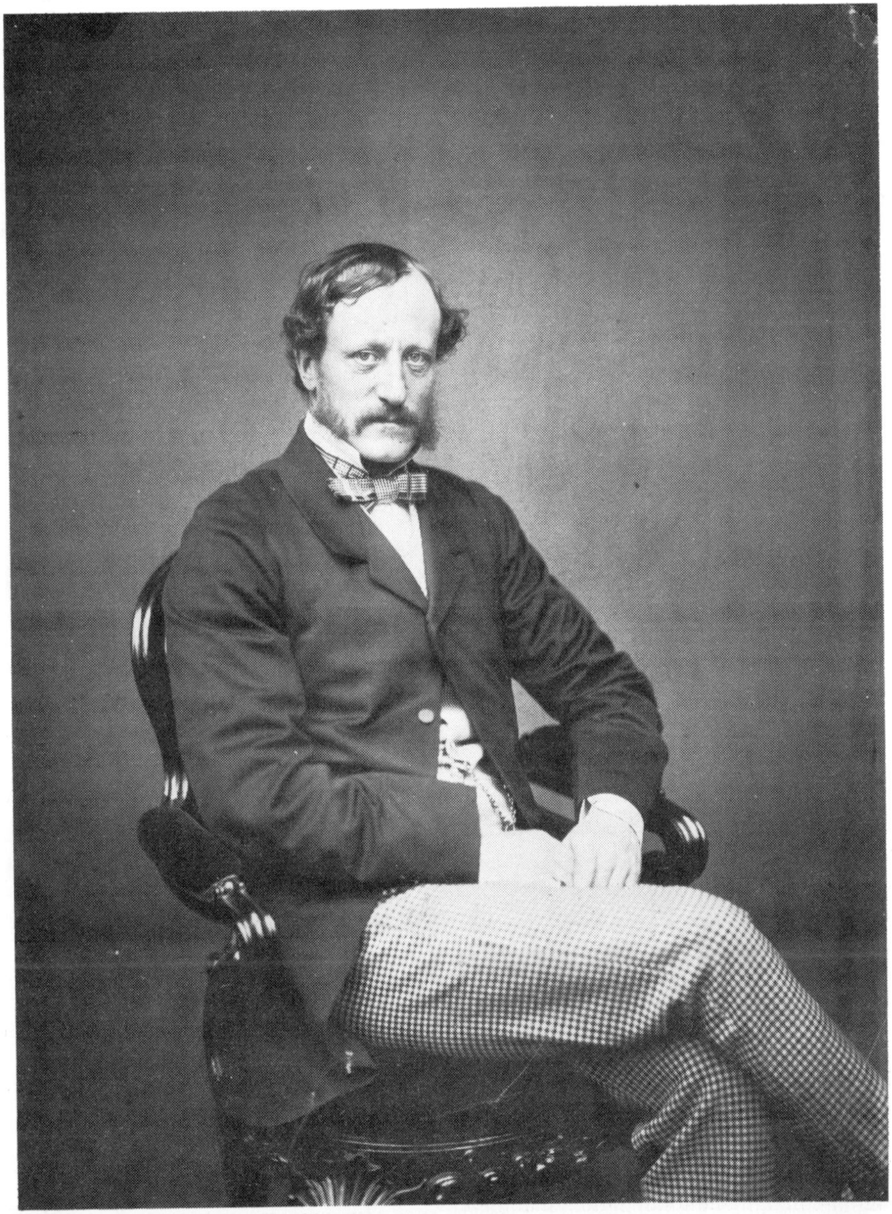

We have come a long way from men in cloth caps nearly a foot wide, from women in mutton sleeves and voluminous skirts covering them to the ankles, when it would have been sheer guesswork to say of one of them, 'She has a fine leg for a button boot.'

It would then have been rare to hear the kind of lament echoed by a Belfast woman shopper about a bargain frock brought home from the sales, 'Ach, it would have fitted me if I could have got it on.'

The white waistcoat for everyday male wear and overcoats reaching to the ground have also joined the long procession of styles that have passed; presumably with no regrets.

Dressed to kill in this Victorian photograph is Lord Edwin Hill Trevor, MP, an Ulster politician of the last century.

The women's ambulance detachment posing with their stretcher might have gone in for the dainty hats advertised in 1914 when they were off duty. Their little sisters might have worn up-to-the minute fashions too, like the outfit below.

Daintiest made-up veils worth 1/11 to 3/6

The newest of the new, in soft hexagon mesh, with shadow flower design, Russian nets with lace pattern, fancy bordered armures. Worth 1/11 to 3/6.

Sale price - each 1/4

Entire stock of veilings at reduced prices

The little Victorian girls in these photographs look very subdued — not surprisingly, in view of the amount of clothing they are wearing. By the 1930s, children's clothes were rather more sensible, as the advertisement below shows. The extract (above right) is from a 1916 edition of the 'Telegraph' and is more concerned with children's health than their clothes. The copy would hardly pass muster by the standards insisted on today, when the claims of advertisers must not be too extravagant.

IF A CHILD IS CROSS, FEVERISH AND SICK,

LOOK, MOTHER! IF TONGUE IS COATED, CLEANSE THE LITTLE BOWELS WITH "CALIFORNIA SYRUP OF FIGS."

Children love this "fruit laxative," and nothing else cleanses the tender stomach, liver and bowels so nicely.

A child simply will not stop playing to empty the bowels, and the result is that they become clogged with waste, the liver becomes sluggish, the stomach is disordered, and then your little one becomes cross, feverish, and does not eat, sleep or behave naturally. Often the breath is bad, and system "stuffy" with a cold; the child has sore throat, stomach-ache, or diarrhœa. Listen, mother! See if tongue is coated, then give a teaspoonful of "California Syrup of Figs," and in a few hours all the constipated waste-matter, sour bile and undigested food pass out of the system, and you have a healthy, playful child again.

Millions of mothers give "California Syrup of Figs" because it is perfectly harmless; children love it, and it never fails to act on the stomach, liver and bowels.

Ask your chemist for a bottle of "California Syrup of Figs," which has full directions for babies, children of all ages and for grown-ups plainly printed on the bottle. Get the genuine made by "California Fig Syrup Company," and sold by all leading chemists, 1s 3d and 2s per bottle. Refuse any other kind with contempt. W903

BARGAIN No. P 29

Just arrived.
A new delivery of our well-known and popular

"Leonard" Jersey Suits

Splendid for the little chap. Made in closely woven stockingette, comprising jersey, cap & knickers. In tan, navy, saxe and cream.

To fit ages 2½ to 6 years. **5/9** per suit complete.
Post 4d.

BARGAIN No. P 37

Marvellous Offers during Sale.

"A.W.G." Kilties.

Jersey and kilt combined. Very durable. Will not shrink. Close woven stockingette, with polo collar. Button at front.

Colours:
Saxe, brown, cardinal and cream.

Length	19 in.	21 in.	23 in.
Sale Prices	2/5½	2/9½	2/11½

Post free.

Back in 1870 a group of the good citizens of Belfast had an outing to the Giant's Causeway and this is how they arranged themselves for a photograph of the occasion. All were members of the Belfast Naturalists' Field Club, which has long been a force in encouraging an interest in the wide range of the Province's natural resources. The Causeway was a particularly popular place for excursions in the 19th century, and the 1874 edition of the 'Telegraph' carried this delightful account of a trip by a humbler section of society. Those were the days when a reporter could really let himself go in his prose style. Doubtless gentlemen of every class found the trousers in the advertisement handy for such expeditions.

WARM SHIRTS and UNDERWEAR

of superior quality and finish offered at attractive prices.

D. Lyle Hall,

19 ROYAL AVENUE.

Holeproof Trousers

Brown herring-bone stripe trousers —Men's and youths. Cloth extra heavy and will wear like moleskin. Clearing all sizes (about a gross altogether) at per pair **4/11**

20-30 YORK STREET.

BOOTS! BOOTS! SHOES! SHOES!

44, 46, & 48 GREAT EDWARD STREET (CONVENIENT TO THE MARKETS).

SKELLY BROTHERS

HAVING PURCHASED A MERCHANT'S STOCK AT A LARGE DISCOUNT OFF PRIME COST, ARE GIVING THE PUBLIC THE FULL BENEFIT.

The Vendor being only a short time in business, the Stock is quite New and from the very best Makers. With this Stock will be offered *special lines*, Cash Purchases in Dresses, Mantles, Millinery, Ready-made Clothing, Hats, Shirts, &c., at startling low prices. 4116

BRASSFOUNDERS' EXCURSION.

On Saturday the members of the Belfast Brassfounders' Trade and Friendly Society held their annual excursion. The place chosen was the Giant's Causeway, where they arrived about 11 o'clock, in company with their wives and sweethearts. After viewing the romantic and imposing scenery for which this far-famed work of Nature is so justly celebrated, and which evidently produced feelings of delight and wonder among the excursionists, dinner was served in Coleman's Hotel in a manner which reflected the utmost credit on this establishment; and the proprietor's endeavours to secure the comfort of his guests met with hearty approval. Mr. Gilbert Cummings presided, and congratulated the members present on the thirty-eighth anniversary of the formation of their association and their prosperous condition. To Messrs. Blair, Ross, Miller, Shand, Brown, and Winnington, votes of thanks were returned for their exertions in promoting the happiness and amusement of the tourists, and in exercising their vocal powers to make the time pass away in an agreeable manner. The party returned home, per car and train, greatly delighted with the day's proceedings.

The old RIC was always smartly turned out as in these pictures of a mounted policeman and recruit John Clark (above). Perhaps it was found that Dri-ped boots, good after 2,000 miles, were useful on the beat.

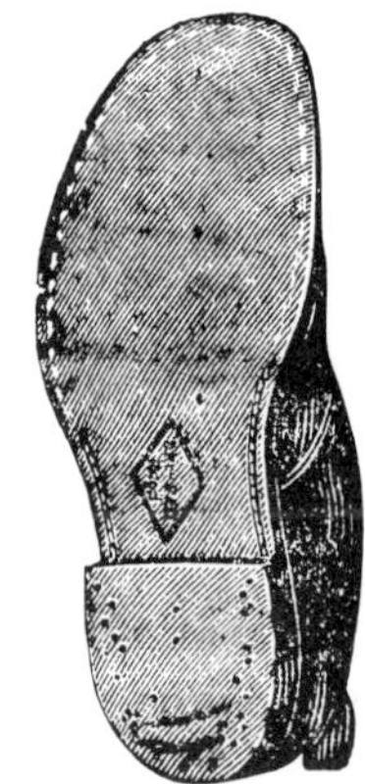

Right Boot.

Original "DRI-PED" sole after 2000 miles

Postman S. Beanland's boots show how much better "DRI-PED" wears than ordinary leather.

Mr. S. Beanland, 12, Parker's Crescent, Chapel Allerton, Leeds, a well-known Leeds Postman, wore a special test pair of boots—the right boot soled with "DRI-PED" and the left boot soled with best ordinary leather.

Mr. Beanland says—

"The "DRI-PED" sole is a great "advantage in wet weather, there "not being that slipping which is "almost always experienced with "the ordinary leather. After being "out all day in the wet, I lay my "boots on their sides, and the wet "runs off the "DRI-PED" leather "and does not soak in. It dries "very quickly and appears to be "impervious to wet."

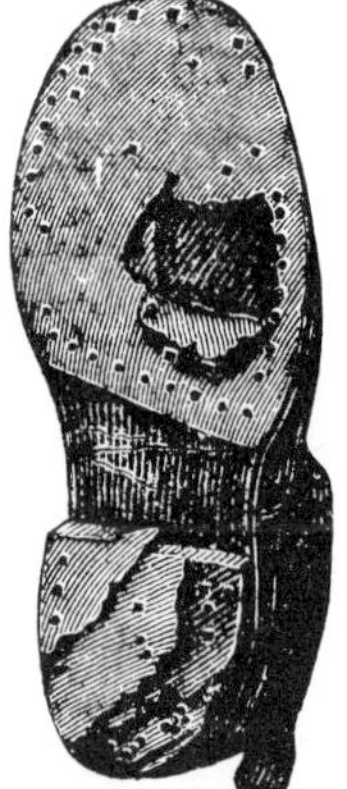

Left Boot.

Second Ordinary sole after 2000 miles

GREAT OFFER OF

50,000 British made caps

to smokers of

CARRERAS'

'CLUBS'

The Best 5 for 2ᴰ. cigarettes

This offer is made because we know that if you will give 'CLUBS' a fair trial you will not smoke an *ordinary* 5 for 2d. cigarette in the future.

'Clubs' are better filled, better made —better value—in fact, the Best 5 for 2d. Cigarettes on the market.

Start smoking 'Clubs' to-day, and save the empty packets.

A CAP IS YOURS FOR ONLY

50 EMPTY 'CLUBS' FIVES PACKETS

When you have collected 50 empty packets, send them, with your name and address.

STATE CLEARLY WHETHER "MEN'S" OR "BOY'S", ALSO SIZE, AND IF PATTERN "A", "B", "C", "D", "E", "F" or "G" IS REQUIRED.

Available in the following sizes:

Send for as many as you like, but each application must be accompanied by 50 empty 'CLUBS' packets.

Send your empty packets to.
'CLUBS', Arcadia Works, Hampstead Road, London, N.W.1

★ THIS OFFER CLOSES ON APRIL 30th 1932

Caps are no longer have the width of those in this photograph of officials of the internment ship Argenta, where internees were held during the 1920 violence. The closing date for the remarkable offer in the advertisement on the left was in the next decade, so it is safe to assume that the gentlemen in the picture did not have smoke themselves insensible to get their fine headgear.

Charm, elegance and exquisite high fashion mark this wedding group in the early years of the century. You may be sure the lady fifth from the left would not be indulging in any wedding cake.

It was called a wayzgoose — in other words a day trip for members of the 'Telegraph's' composing room staff in 1913. A white waistcoat was acceptable wear for the event. Perhaps they got their smart outfits from Gideon Baird.

GIDEON BAIRD

INVITES THE ATTENTION OF HIS FRIENDS AND THE PUBLIC TO HIS Stock o

HATS AND CAPS,

Comprising all the Newest Styles and Shapes for the present season.

The prices will be the same as formerly, care being taken that the Hats, notwithstanding; the advance in the price of Silk, will be of the same sterling Quality, Brilliancy and Colour.

LINCOLN & BENNETT'S HATS,

CHRISTIE'S CELEBRATED FELT HATS.

BAIRD'S CELEBRATED 10s 6d HAT IS SPECIALLY RECOMMENDED.

GET YOUR STRAW HAT AT GIDEON BAIRD'S, MAYFAIR—NEW SEASON'S STOCK, COMPRISING UPWARDS OF 4,000 HATS, NOW READY. SEE THE SPECIAL BON-TON STYLE AT THREE-AND-SIX.

BORDER MUSIC COMEDY.

SIR THOMAS BEECHAM'S IRISH JIG.

ORCHESTRA PLAYS IN STREET

WHILE OFFICERS SEARCH CASES.

A remarkable experience of Sir Thomas Beecham and his London Philharmonic Orchestra at Carrickarnon on the Border.

Sir Thomas and his musicians were ordered out of their buses near Dundalk and all were requested to open up their cases to see if they had anything excisable.

Sir Thomas protested that they had no firearms, but his protests were unavailing and, assembling the orchestra in the street, he conducted them through a classical piece while the zealous Customs officers searched the cases.

At the finish of the orchestral effort, Sir Thomas, to the amusement of his party, humorously gave a few steps of Irish jig in the middle of the street.

"The music," said Sir Thomas in an interview, "was a mixture of everything, but good enough to dance an Irish jig to. The audience seemed most appreciative—the most amusing audience I have ever performed before.

"They comprised old women—about a dozen—a few cats and a few barking dogs, and so the fun continued until the Customs men realised we were only travelling musicians."

Unlikely if the 'Tailor and Cutter' would give any marks for style to the members of the Boundary Commission, here photographed in 1924 at Armagh (left) and somewhere in the field (above) when they were preparing a report on the line the Irish Border should follow. Let's hope the turkeys were satisfied, even if Sir Thomas Beecham was not.

Lord Craigavon, Northern Ireland's first Prime Minister, suffers the rigours of court dress as he sets out with his wife for a State function in London. Her ladyship, looking elegantly at ease, might have posed for one of the 'Telegraph's' fashion drawings in earlier years.

FOR AFTERNOON WEAR.

The Travelling Yesterdays

Sunny Day at the Junction

It is the turn of the century and the horse trams cast their shadows alongside the stand where jaunting cars and a hansom await a fare. There isn't a car in sight. Not even a yellow line can be seen, nor a traffic warden with notebook eagerly at the ready. Just a quiet, leisurely day.

It is a far cry from the time when it cost only twopence to travel in Belfast by horse tram, no matter how far you were going. If you preferred the open top deck it cost only a penny. Nevertheless the lady of whom it was said 'She was sitting in the tram with her mouth open like a two lb. jampot' could just as readily be a passenger in a pay-as-you-enter bus. Today's cars have brought their own revolution to traffic conditions. Yet even the car isn't what it was.

Looking more like an old time stage coach, a horse bus waits at Castle Junction during the 1870s.

By the turn of the century the transport revolution was under way, and up-to-the-minute buses like this one were taking over. But there's still a stage-coach air about the solid tyred wheels.

The passing years saw marked changes in the styling of trams. The decorative iron work on the 1905 tram below has disappeared from the streamlined 1920s model on the left. Those were the gay old days when visitors from Ballymena were apt to look askance at the upper deck, describing it as 'the laft'.

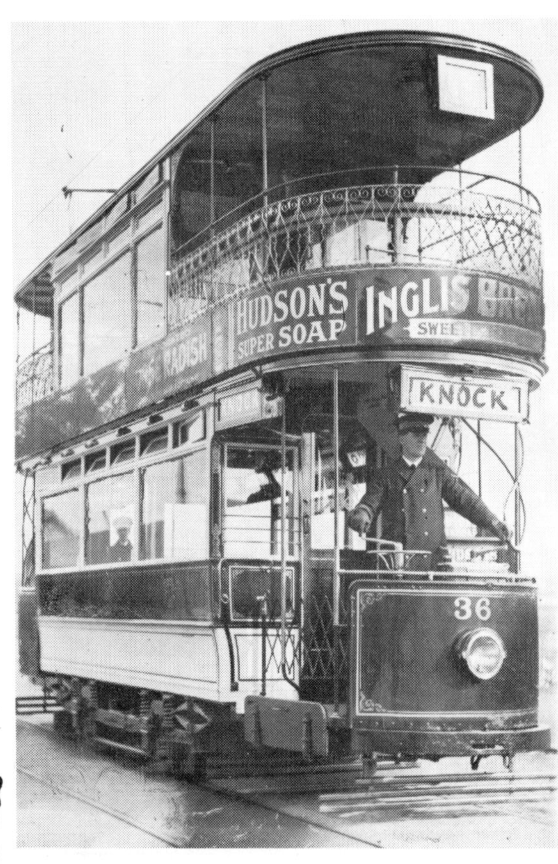

BELFAST TRAMCAR IN COLLISION.

In Donegall Street, Belfast as people were proceeding to business about half-past nine, an exciting incident was witnessed in Donegall Street, at Talbot Street corner, when a down-town tramcar collided with a heavy steam traction machine, which was conveying a heavy load of animal feeding stuffs.

The motorman, who applied his brakes with great promptitude, was seriously injured about the legs, and was taken to hospital by the fire brigade ambulance. His name is Joseph Hunter, and he is reported to be making fair progress For almost an hour the street traffic in this busy thoroughfare of the city was practically held up, both vehicles being inter-locked and the front of the tramcar almost a complete wreck.

The injured motorman, Hunter, who resides in Hillview Street, is under treatment in the Royal Victoria Hospital, his injuries being described as contusions on the body and legs. He had a miraculous and narrow escape from death.

The day finally came when the last tram ticket was punched, and the friendly clatter they made as they racketed along their rails was still. They're still sadly missed by an older generation of travellers.

129 1907
BELFAST CITY TRAMWAYS.

1d.

This Ticket is only available on the Car on which it is issued, and will only serve to convey the passenger as far on his way as that Car goes. It is subject to the List of Fares exhibited in the Car.

14 566
BELFAST ST. TRAMWAYS CO.

FARE - 1d

This Ticket is available for a SINGLE journey only on the Car where issued, and will only serve to carry the passenger as far on his way as that Car goes.

BETWEEN
Donegall Rd. & Mount Pleasant
Castle Junc. & Cliftonville St.
Castle Junc. & Westbourne St.
Westbourne St & Magee's Rd.
Holywood Arches & Knock
Castle Junc. & Dublin St.
Oxford St. & South Parade
Castle Junc. & Dunville Pk. Jn.
Durham St. & Springfield Bdg.
College Gardens & Balmoral
Castle Junction & following
10 points:—
College Gdns., Springfield Rd.,
Leopold St., Shankhill Graveyd
Cavehill Rd., M'[illegible] Cor.
Mile [illegible] St., Beer's Bdge. Rd.
Agincourt Av., [illegible] Gdns.

THE DUNLOP RUBBER CO., LTD., FOUNDERS OF T

UMATIC TYRE INDUSTRY, 41 Chichester Street, Belfast.

The grand old gentleman on the bike is J B Dunlop, the Ulsterman who invented the pneumatic tyre, photographed at the annual meet of the Irish Cyclists' Old Timers Fellowship in Dublin, 1918. The company's publicity in earlier years was very imaginative — even Dunlop's imposing appearance was turned to good account.

The Dunlop Rubber Co., Ld., Birmingham, England.

Nairobi House, Sixth Avenue, Nairobi, B.E.A.

Dear Sirs,
In the interests of motor cyclists generally, I think the following remarkable instance of the durability of your belts should be made known.

On my 4¼ "B.S.A." Sidecar combination a 1-in. Dunlop belt has done 2,000 miles in six months over rotten roads in mountain country without needing to be tightened, and its ends are perfect, and the fastener is as if it were inserted to-day.

The performance is the more remarkable when you remember the disintegrating effect the equatorial sunlight has on ordinary rubber.

With compliments,
I am, dear Sirs,
Yours faithfully,
(Signed) A. H. Spencer-Palmer.

Buses operated by private companies such as the one on the right served the public well for many years. Gradually the smaller companies were taken over by larger groups. Public bodies, like Belfast Corporation whose very first motor bus is shown below, also joined the field. The early days of fierce competition between the smaller companies had their advantages: if you missed a bus and one of the company's inspectors happened to be passing in his car he would give you a lift to catch it up rather than let a rival company **get** *your fare.*

THE BEST WAY TO TRAVEL

Preliminary Announcement

THE Travelling Public is hereby notified that the Service owned and operated by **D. McATEE & SONS, Greencastle Street, KILKEEL,** and running between

BELFAST — NEWCASTLE — KILKEEL;
NEWRY — KILKEEL;
KILKEEL — MASSFORTH, etc.,

has been purchased by the **Belfast Omnibus Company, Limited,** and will be taken over and operated by them as and from **WEDNESDAY, 1st MARCH, 1933.**

JAMES McCREA, M.Inst.T.,
Managing Director.

The strongest runner in the great transport race turned out to be the motor car. These two splendid vehicles are owned by the Wilson family of Portadown. Top is the 1911 Standard used by Emily Pankhurst during her suffragette campaign. Below is a Rolls Royce Silver Ghost from the late Twenties. And hold you horses — the furious driver in the cutting below ran foul of the traffic laws in the 1870s, before such vehicles as these were thought of.

FURIOUS DRIVING,

A car-driver, named Wm. Dodds, was charged by Sub-Constable M'Kechney with having been drunk in charge of a horse and car, and with having furiously driven the same. The constable said he arrested the prisoner yesterday for being drunk while in charge of his horse and car. He was also furiously driving his horse. Mr. O'Donnell—What rate was he driving? Witness—I would say about nine or ten miles per hour. Mr. O'Donnell—We must do something to stop this furious driving in the streets of Belfast. You must go to jail one month.

As the years went by cars — like this 1926 Morris Oxford Tourer — became more and more dashing. So did drivers, like the man in 'Radiator's' report in 1933. More staid and functional vehicles, like the 1945 Austin van, had their place too.

ULSTER MOTOR TOPICS

SHOCK A DRIVER GOT

POLICE SAID HE WAS DOING 130 M.P.H.

LIMIT IN PROSECUTIONS

(By " RADIATOR.")

Motorists from time to time have some queer experiences with the police.

Designed for long-life dependability

THE NEW

AUSTIN "TEN" VAN

Austin engineering, plus war-time experience, give this Van an engine packed with power — an engine more efficient, more economical, more dependable than ever. Every detail is planned for performance — and built to last. The van has a capacity of 120 cubic feet, and will carry loads of various goods up to 10 cwt. It is as comfortable to handle as a private car. Ask for full details—you'll be glad you did.

Price at works, in grey priming £284.

Austin Distributors for Ulster:

HARRY FERGUSON (Motors) LTD.

Telephone: Belfast 25444. DONEGALL SQ. EAST, BELFAST.

The AA man, with his goggles, side-car and smart salute, brought a touch of chivalry to the roads. Less gallant was the girl-chasing Baby Austin reported in the 'Telegraph' in the 1930s. Pretty girls and cars seem to go naturally together, as in the 1964 picture of a Mini and the first Austin Seven to reach Belfast in 1924.

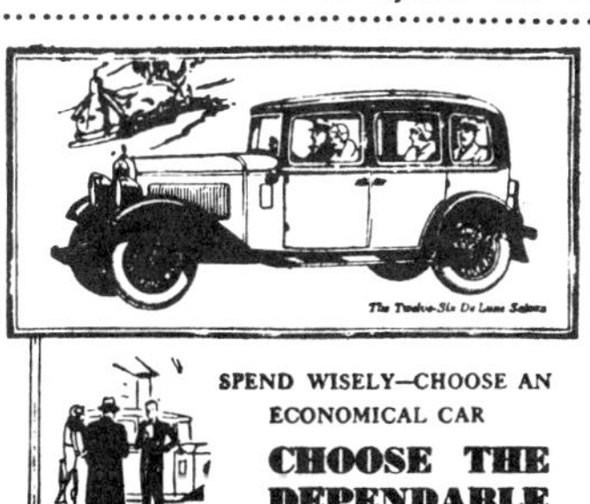

SPEND WISELY—CHOOSE AN ECONOMICAL CAR

CHOOSE THE DEPENDABLE AUSTIN!

Choose a car that is economical to run, that is built to endure, that does not require frequent servicing. *Choose an Austin—the car of outstanding dependability.* You then will be assured of motoring that is as light on your pocket as it is satisfying in performance and freedom from care.

Every model in the new range shows some new and striking feature, which we invite you to see for yourself at our showrooms . . .

Superb upholstery and lavish equipment in the Twenty models . . . new steel bodies in the Sixteen and Twelve-Six lines . . . greater roominess and better finish in the new Sevens.

And with all these improvements, with Austin's outstanding dependability—*these cars are reduced in price.*

Call round—inspect any model—you will be under no obligation.

Seven Models from £118 to £128; Twelve-Four from £268 to £288; Twelve-Six from £198 to £225; Sixteens from £290 to £350; Twenty from £498 to £575. Dunlop tyres, Triplex glass throughout and chromium finish standard.

SEE YOUR *Austin* DEALER FIRST

Austin Dealers in Ulster:

ARMAGH. D. H. M'DOWELL & CO.
BELFAST. VICTOR LTD., 1 Bedford St.
O. D. CARS, LTD., Antrim Road.
KNOCK CYCLE & MOTOR CO., Upper N'Ards Road.
A. R. ELLIOTT, University Street.
BALLYMENA. DICKEY & PINKERTON.
W. D. MONTGOMERY (SUB).
BANGOR. R. J. HOOKE
S. C. TAYLOR (SUB).
BALLYCASTLE. J. W. M'CAUGHAN.
COLERAINE. T. MacFARLANE & SONS.
COOKSTOWN. T. & C. M'GUCKEN.
DONAGHADEE & N'ARDS. H. & J. M'GIMPSEY.
ENNISKILLEN. T. E. WATSON.
LONDONDERRY. THOMPSON EDWARDS MOTOR CO. LTD.
LISBURN. J. W. ASHE.
LARNE. JOHN A. MAGEE.
NEWRY. ROWLAND & HARRIS, LTD.
OMAGH. QUIGLEY & CO.
PORTADOWN. RICHARD HEWITT.

SOLE ULSTER DISTRIBUTORS:

HARRY FERGUSON, Ltd.
DONEGALL SQUARE - - - BELFAST.

"BABY AUSTIN CHASING GIRLS."

ALARM NEAR WARRENPOINT.

REFERENCE IN GAME PROSECUTION.

"There was great talk in the country about a Baby Austin chasing and frightening girls," said a defendant in a game prosecution at Warrenpoint Petty Sessions.

"Did they get the Baby Austin yet?" queried the clerk.

The Belfast Central Railway train above was photographed in 1880. The Portstewart train below was operated by the Northern Counties Committee. Its passenger accommodation seems to have been hi-jacked from a passing horse-tram.

TEMPORARY PASSENG

MONDAY, 6th FEBRU

FROM BELFAST

To Lisburn—7-10, 7-50, 9-30, 10-0, 1
a.m., 12-15,
3-15, 4-20,
6-10 and 6-1
To Portadown-
5-5, 6-10, 7-
To Banbridge—
6-15, 7-30 a
To Armagh —
and 7-15 p.
To Antrim E
Crumlin, 6-
Trains and Sp
from Great V

OMAGH a

10-30 a.m.—Or
giving conn
Bus ex Lo
1-45 p.m.—Oma
8-30 p.m. — O
giving conn
Bus ex Lo
8-40 a.m. — E
connecting with 10-15 a.m.
Omagh to Londonderry.

WITH

TRAI

SUNDAY, 5

THERE wi
TO-M
The Tempor
resumed on M
MA

U. T. A.

RETURN

1798

Belfast (G.V.

TO

FINAGHY

SECOND CLAS

Valid Three Mon

This Ticket is

conveyance of

R B

& OMNIBUS SERVICE

until Further Notice.

TO BELFAST

Lisburn—7-6, 8-5, 8-25, 8-26, 8-35,
, 12-15, 12-40,
3-40, 4-45, 5-15,

S
COUNTIES
MMITTEE

7-45, 8-55, 11-30
m.

7-45, 8-25, 8-35
2-45 p.m.

WAL

VICE

RY, 1933.

RAINS run
lay).
vice will be

R

5 a.m., 1-15 and
ill 5-30, Porta-
. 5-50, arriving

-7-45 a.m. from
from Crumlin.

nnibuses start
tations.

DUNGANNON

to Dungannon,
9-3 a.m. Bus
ast.

p.m.—Cookstown to Dungannon,
nnecting with 6-3 p.m. Bus

U. T. A.
TICKET
Finaghy
TO
LFA (GV)
ECOND CLASS
Fare 1/-
ubject to "The
rs Conditions"
st
0699

The train at Helen's Bay station, above, was operated by yet another company, the Belfast and County Down Railway. The picture below shows the end of the line for many of the Ulster Transport Authority's locomotives, which were auctioned in 1965. The collector of the two tickets must have been a politician as well as a railway enthusiast.

Harry Ferguson, the outstanding Ulster pioneer of aviation and motor vehicles, is seen above in one of his early aeroplanes. Nowadays he is best remembered for the development of the Ferguson tractor. Planes were a great inspiration to advertisers in earlier years.

Water transport also came on apace. An excursion party is enjoying a day out on the 'Lough Neagh Queen' in 1905 (left). But it wasn't all plain sailing as the shot below of the 'Davaar' on the rocks at Groomsport in 1895 shows. The children seem to think white pinafores were appropriate dress for the occasion.

AMUSEMENTS.

New York Cinema—To-day
YORK STREET.

A TRAGEDY OF THE SEA

A Thrilling Story, in Three Parts.

The Showtime Yesterdays

To an older generation show-time spelt the long gone Theatre Royal and the Carl Rosa Opera Company. It meant the music hall days of the Alhambra and the Empire, besides films at such cinemas as the Panopticon.

But time marches on and we had the era when show-time meant the big band shows, rock and roll, and such groups as the Beatles and the Rolling Stones.

Down the years the show circuit brought all the top names to the city, from Gigli to Dame Nellie Melba, from Irving Berlin to Dickie Valentine.

The New
ALHAMBRA
THEATRE
OF VARIETIES

. . . TWO . . .
PERFORMANCES NIGHTLY
7 and 9.
Saturdays :—6-45 and 8-45.

Ten Star Turns
at . . .
Each Performance.

PRICES OF ADMISSION:
3d., 6d., 1/- & 1/6.

General Manager: H. T. DOWNS.

The old Alhambra programme recalls the great days of the music hall, when, 'the elite of the variety profession' entertained Belfast citizens twice nightly all the year round.

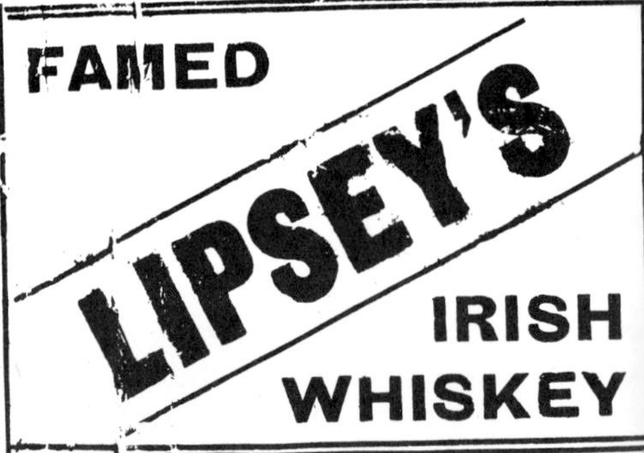

Down Smithfield.

Written, Composed, and Sung with big success by GEO. PRINCE.

You should never interfere if you hear a copper sing, Down Smithfield.
For if you do he's bound to put your eye-ball in a sling, Down Smithfield.
I'm looking for a josser, he's a terror, so I hear,
He's always on the make-haste, and he wants to bite your ear,
All day in Paddy's market, and all night he's mopping beer, Down Smithfield.

The Alhambra, famous Belfast music hall and a North Street landmark. The dearest seats in the house in 1903 were 1s 6d; the cheapest were 3d. Alongside are some advertisements for Belfast variety shows over the years. I'm not too sure if 'Maciste', who knocked them in the aisles at the Crumlin Picture House in 1916, was a live act or a film. He was certainly great value at 2½d a time.

Theatre Royal,

BELFAST.

Monday, Nov. 27th, 1905,

FOR SIX NIGHTS AND ONE MATINEE

Special Morning Performance Friday, Dec. 1st, at 2

"FAUST."

35th Year without a break of Her Late Majesty's Servants the World-Renowned

ROYAL

CARL ROSA OPERA COMPANY

The Oldest Opera Co. in the World

Full Orchestra

Chorus and Ballet.

The entertainment scene in Ulster has catered for all types of audience — high, low and middle-brow. Opera has had a specially fine tradition. Classical music, too, has never failed to draw an appreciative turnout. Left is an early Belfast opera programme; below a review of a Festival of Britain concert in 1951. The critic is less than enthusiastic about the performance.

A rather long concert but interesting

THE first of three Festival Concerts by the City of Belfast Orchestra was given in the Ulster Hall on Tuesday evening. The burst of belated sunshine must have called many people to their gardens, which was a pity, as we had a good concert, rather too long but interesting.

Beniamino Gigli, the great tenor, (above) goes through some of his fan mail in the Grand Central Hotel when he was in Belfast to sing in the King's Hall in 1954. On his right is his manager. Gigli was asked whom he considered to be the world's greatest tenor. His reply, 'Sometimes I hear one. Sometimes I hear another. But I prefer Gigli.' Another great singer, the Irish tenor John McCormack (left), sang at many Belfast concerts and never failed to draw big audiences.

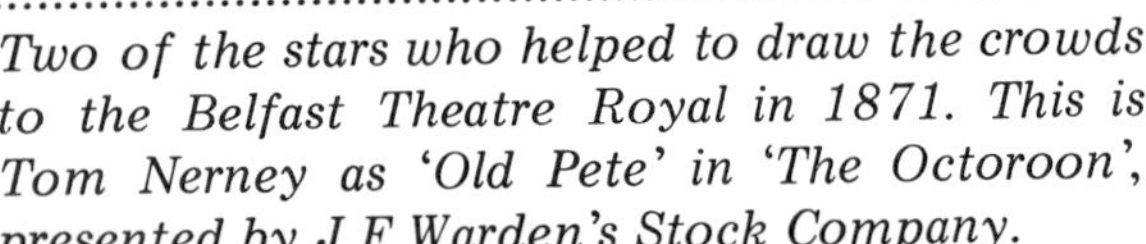

Two of the stars who helped to draw the crowds to the Belfast Theatre Royal in 1871. This is Tom Nerney as 'Old Pete' in 'The Octoroon', presented by J F Warden's Stock Company.

An actor who is credited only with the name 'Adam' in the role of 'Jacob McCloskey' in the same production. At first glance he gives the impression of having gone to the same school of acting as Ben Turpin.

Ulster writers and actors have made their own special contribution to drama over the years. St John Ervine, perhaps the best-known of the Province's modern playwrights, reads over a typescript in his Devon home. Right is an advertisement from the Thirties for a film version of one of his plays.

This century has seen the rise, the hey-day and — to an extent — the eclipse of the film industry. Ulster people have been great film fans ever since the golden days of silent four reelers at the Panopticon. One of Ulster's most notable contributions to Hollywood was Errol Flynn, son of a Queen's University professor, but better known as Robin Hood and the man who won wars galore single-handed.

ANTRIM **Capitol** ROAD

All This Week—1-30, 3-50, 6-10, 8-30:

ERROL FLYNN

OLIVIA DE HAVILLAND in

CAPTAIN BLOOD

¶ *TO-DAY,*
TUESDAY AND WEDNESDAY

LONDON FILM

The Morals of Weybury

Adapted from the famous play 'The Hypocrites' by Henry Arthur Jones

FOUR REELS

With ELISABETH RISDON in the leading role

THIS celebrated play, in which there are so many fine scenes and interesting situations, was quite the biggest success of the year in which it was produced. In adapting it to the screen the London Film Co. have scored a brilliant triumph. A film drama of the highest order and one you should on no account miss

¶ ALSO

FULL PROGRAMME COMEDY AND INTEREST

The Picture House

Royal Avenue, Belfast.

PANOPTICON—To-day

A SUPERB METRO Play—

"Black Fear"

(Miss Cocaine on a Mission from the Devil).

A Janitor's Wife's Temptation

(Triangle-Keystone), making Model Models, all thumbs and all up! &c., &c.

Tinkling the ivories on the left is Irving Berlin, who appeared at Belfast Opera House in 1942 at a show for American troops. During his visit he learned that when a Belfast parent warns a youngster, 'If you don't put that down I'll give it to you,' the words don't mean exactly what they say. Berlin was duly impressed. Inevitably he played one of his many famous tunes, 'Over There'. War-time was the hey-day of dance halls and clubs.

Short & Harland's Machine Shop
(Centre 30) Grand Repeat Dance, 9—1.
NEW CONGA CLUB BALLROOM, Agnes St. Cabaret. Spot Prizes and Surprises. Guest Artists. 2/6, 3/-

EMBASSY 20950
"ON THE BEAM"
9—3 **CLUB**

The MANHATTAN CLUB
5 CORN MARKET.
St. Patrick's Night GRAND CABARET BALL, 9—2. Reserve your tables early.
Phone 250871.

CLUB ESTAIRE
ST. PATRICK'S NIGHT BALL,
Saturday, 17th March.
Admission by Ticket Only. Formal.

FLORAL HALL, Bellevue
DANCING
EVERY NIGHT .... 7-30—10-30

The big bands of the post-war years never failed to include Ulster in the circuit when they went on tour. One name always associated with the big band era was Jack Hylton, a polished performer. He is seen here with the band's front row.

Radio was another new entertainment medium in this century. Serials like 'Mrs Lally's Lodgers' by Jack Loudan were very popular with Ulster listeners. Familiar faces at this 1958 rehearsal for the show are Colin Blakely, sharing his script on the right, and James Ellis, later of 'Z Cars', on the left. A great favourite with everyone was 'The McCooeys': Joe Tomelty, who wrote the script, is pictured, left, discussing a feature film in 1954 with the BBC personality, Richard Dimbleby.

Radio

NORTHERN IRELAND (261 metres)

5-55 p.m., The Weather. **6-0,** News. **6-15,** Northern Ireland News. **6-20,** News from the North of England. **6-25,** Sport. **6-30,** "The M'Cooeys." **6-50,** Traditional Music. **7-0,** Northern Ireland Quiz Team at Bushmills, Co. Antrim. **7-30,** Search for a Song. **8-0,** Lizbeth Webb in "Threesome." **8-15,** Merino: The story of Australian wool. **9-0,** News. **9-15,** The World To-day. **9-30,** We Beg to Differ. **10-0,** A Stake in Society: Possession and the Law, by two barristers. **10-20,** London Czech Trio. **10-45,** To-day in Parliament. **11-0,** News. **11-3 app.,** Close.

LIGHT PROGRAMME (1,500. 247m.)

6-15 p.m., Your Music Club. **6-45,** The Archers: A story of country folk. **7-0,** News and Radio Newsreel. **7-25,** Sport. **7-30,** The Mounties. **8-0,** Stories. **8-15,** Re-

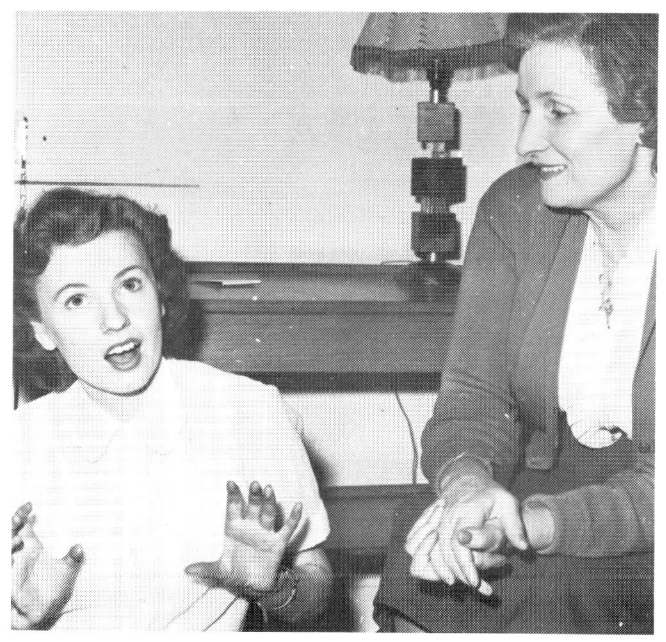

Pop singers, skiffle, traditional jazz all came to the fore in the Fifties. Belfast girl Ruby Murray is pictured with her mother at home in 1955. Sales of her record 'Softly, Softly' reached a fantastic total. Also at home with his mother in Roslyn Street in 1961 is national heart throb Ronnie Carroll. Another popular singer of those years who came from Ulster was Ottilie Patterson, who sang with Chris Barber's jazz band. Pop singer Dickie Valentine always got a great reception in Belfast — he called it 'the fornenst city'. He was killed in a car crash in 1971.

BELFAST'S FIRST JAZZ FESTIVAL

3 Nights of Jazz at Floral Hall, Bellevue

On MONDAY, TUESDAY and WEDNESDAY,

the 14th, 15th and 16th OCTOBER, 1957, with

CHRIS BARBER AND HIS BAND

AND OTTILIE PATTERSON

DANCING MONDAY and TUESDAY, 8-0 p.m.—11-30. DANCING WEDNESDAY, 8-0 p.m.—12-0 midnight. Admission, 5/-.

Tickets on sale at THE GRAMOPHONE SHOP, 16 Donegall Square North, and ATLANTIC RECORDS, 69 High Street.

LATE TRANSPORT AVAILABLE

The late Fifties saw the birth of a new kind of music — rock and roll. Some of the superstars of that era, such as Elvis Presley, are still great names today. Pictured above is Bill Haley, another of the rock and roll kings. He was attempting to revive interest in this type of music when he visited Belfast with his Comets in 1968. But the Floral Hall was only half filled. Rock and roll, and the pop groups of the Sixties were marked by the wild scenes at their concerts. Mick Jagger, pictured right with a Belfast fan, and his group the Rolling Stones, got that kind of reception wherever they went.

The Beatles

SCREAMING GIRLS GREET BEATLES

4 YOUNG MEN TAKE BELFAST BY STORM

THERE was never anything like it here before—and there probably will never be anything like it again.

That is, unless the £5,000 a week Beatles decide to return to Belfast, the city whose teenage population broke out last night in almost unbelievable scenes of mass-hysteria.

Four thousand people saw them—and six thousand outside wanted to see them. They were not disappointed. Surrounded by a bodyguard of a dozen policemen they walked out of the front door of the ABC cinema and into their chauffeur-driven limousine.

They had given two shows, playing and singing tremendous Liverpool Beat music—but little of it was heard above the screaming "chorus."

But the greatest of them all were the four talented young men on the right. Like the rest of the world, Belfast gave them a tumultuous welcome.

Empire bows out

Now 1,859 TV sets in Coleraine area

A CONSIDERABLE increase in the number of television sets in the Coleraine area was reported by the head postmaster (Mr. J, Torrens) at a meeting of the Coleraine Post Office Advisory Committee. There were now 1,859 sets an increase of 772 within a year,

In the Fifties TV, the last — so far — of the twentieth century's entertainment innovations, was capturing the headlines. Undoubtedly it helped bring about the demise of old theatres like the Empire in Belfast.

The Sporting Yesterdays

Pedestrianism — walking to you — was a great sport with the Victorians. Gruelling endurance races, similar to the dance marathons of the Thirties, were undertaken by professionals. The competitors in this go-as-you-please race from Belfast to Lurgan in 1903 were clearly not planning on going by plimsoll the entire way. Shorts were definitely worn longer at that time. The only member of the group in a collar and tie is Andrew Stewart, editor of the 'Telegraph', which sponsored the race.

Golf at Portrush is no longer as leisurely — or exclusive — as it was a century or so ago. Television has given sport a dimension it lacked when Linfield and Celtic supporters went to 'the match' by horse tram.

And we have come a long way since boxing tournaments at Belfast's Chapel Fields, when the spectators sat on wooden forms, and one impatient customer, peeved at the late start of the big fight, once cried out angrily, 'Hurry up there. The mugs is on the shelves.'

Whatever the activity, however — soccer, rugby, athletics, motor cycling, boxing — the laurels of greatness have come to exponents from the Province.

VICTORIA DOG RACING GROUNDS.

MERSEY STREET.

TO-MORROW, at **3** p.m.,

AND

TUESDAY, 3rd March.

CELTIC PARK.

CITY CUP MATCH.

GLENTORAN

v.

CELTIC.

TO-MORROW. KICK-OFF. **3-30.**

Golf at Portrush in the late Nineties was nothing if not elegant. The four-ball on the left approaching the second hole has a stylishness of its own. The caddies give the impression of being barefoot. In the scene below the cows appear to have a degree of curiosity in the lady about to putt on the Ballycastle links. Women golfers at the turn of the century were enthusiasts for being warmly clad.

Ulster has made its own special contribution to the great names of golf and is still doing so. Above are two famous exponents of the game. Left is Jimmy Bruen whose grip broke all the rules. Swinging his way into the record books is, right, the great Fred Daly, the first Irishman to win the British open championship. In the same year, 1947, he also won the match play title.

For years Linfield (above) and Celtic (below) dominated the soccer scene in Belfast. They were the nursery of some of the game's most famous players. It was Celtic which made an American tour in 1949 and defeated Scotland in New York in a match still talked about with awe. Below is the Linfield team of 1915-1916 one of its most noteworthy sides. Linfield won the Irish cup more than 30 times — a record no other Irish League side has equalled. Football supporters, past as well as present, showed their enthusiasm with their vocal chords — the cutting below is from the early Thirties.

NOVEL PROSECUTION.

LINFIELD SUPPORTERS' SING-SONG

ON A CATHERWOOD BUS

WHEN PASSING THROUGH LURGAN.

Two bus drivers employed by Messrs. H. M. S. Catherwood were to-day in the Belfast Summons Court, before Mr. H. Toppin, R.M., prosecuted by District-Inspector Hamilton, for allowing a number of Linfield supporters to indulge in "loud singing or outcry," the particular ditty complained of being "Here, here, the Blues are here."

They were Hamilton M'Clements, Thorndyke Street (off Templemore Avenue), and Jos. Bowden, Harkness Parade (Mersey Street district).

Mr. N. Tughan defended.

Police evidence was given that as the two buses passed through Lurgan there was a sing-song in progress.

Mr. Tughan said that in cases like this, where excursion buses were employed, there was no conductor. The driver could hardly be held responsible for the heartiness of his passengers.

M'Clements said he was taking the party home after a social evening following the match. His whole time was taken up with driving and he knew nothing about what had happened until he was stopped. In his driver's seat he did not know what was going on behind him.

Northern Ireland reached the quarter finals of the World Cup in Sweden in 1958. The team's captain, Danny Blanchflower, is shown leading his side on to the field and, in a more relaxed mood, interested in souvenir miniatures of the team. The cutting below recalls Danny's younger brother, Jackie, whose great promise as a footballer was cut short when he was injured in the Munich air disaster earlier in 1958.

MATT BUSBY'S 'COLTS' SHOULD BE ATTRACTION

THE coming visit of the Manchester United youth team, which manager Matt Busby is bringing to Belfast on May 9, has aroused keen interest (writes "Wanderer"), and already all the centre stand tickets at Grosvenor Park have been sold out.

The team will include right-half Whitefoot, who made his debut in the United First Division side at the age of 16, and has played several games recently.

Centre-half Jones, Barnsley and England schoolboy international, and left-half Jackie Blanchflower (brother of Danny), an Irish schoolboy international, of whom many English sportswriters predict a bright future, will also travel.

Tommy Ritchie, the former Bangor outside-right, who is now a centre-forward and earning a good Press, will lead the attack.

The opposition is to be provided by the players of the Summer League team, Lomond Star, who made such a stir in winning the Clark Groves Cup at Strandtown last year.

Members of the Irish Rugby XV which won the Triple Crown in 1947-48. Holding the ball is the captain, Karl Mullen.

IRELAND'S SATURDAY NIGHT, MARCH 13, 1948.

IRELAND'S TRIPLE CROWN TRIUMPH: HISTORIC GAME IN PICTURES

In the Boxing World

St. Patrick's

Bands and Bandsmen.

Record Entry

Among the most exciting events of the Northern Ireland sporting calendar are the motor cycle races — particularly the Ulster Grand Prix run over the Dundrod circuit. On the right in the picture above is Northern Ireland's Artie Bell, shown with his colleagues from the Norton team after the 1950 Tourist Trophy race in the Isle of Man. Stanley Woods, left, who rode in the first Ulster Grand Prix in 1922, scored many successes in a long career, mostly on Nortons. He won ten TT races. Few starts look more spectacular than that of a motor cycle race. The picture overleaf, which shows the start of an Ulster Grand Prix 125 cc event, captures all the atmosphere of 'They're off'.

Dundrod record

THE RESULTS

125 C.C. CLASS

Fastest lap J. Redman — 4 mins. 38.6 secs. — 95.83 m.p.h.

3
3
29
29
17

19
19
17

LOUGH NEAGH SPEEDING

OVER 100 MILES AN HOUR

MISS ENGLAND BEATS RECORD

THROTTLE HALF OPEN

A speed of approximately 100 miles per hour was attained by Miss England II. on her final trial on Lough Neagh.

The monster speed-boat was on the Lough for almost half-an-hour, and at the conclusion of the run Mr. Kaye Don, who piloted the boat, said it behaved magnificently.

The first Ulster Tourist car race was run on the Ards circuit in 1928. It attracted crowds of more than 100,000 and drew the world's top drivers. It continued on the circuit until 1936, later being run on the Dundrod circuit. On the facing page is the 'Telegraph's' dramatic shot of the first race, and a picture of its winner, Kaye Don — who achieved still more fame when a mineral water firm named one of its drinks after him. Having a cup of tea before that first 1928 race in the photograph above are, left to right, Lord Curzon, Captain (later Sir Malcolm) Campbell, and Harry Ferguson, the great Ulster pioneer of car design. Kaye Don, like Sir Malcolm Campbell and his son Donald, was well-known as a speed champion on water as well as land. His feats on Lough Neagh were reported in a 1931 edition of the 'Telegraph'.

Rinty Monaghan (right) embraces his opponent Jackie Patterson after defeating Patterson for the world fly-weight title in the King's Hall in 1948. Within two years Rinty had relinquished four titles and retired from the ring. Usually after a fight he added an extra ingredient to the proceedings by bursting into song.

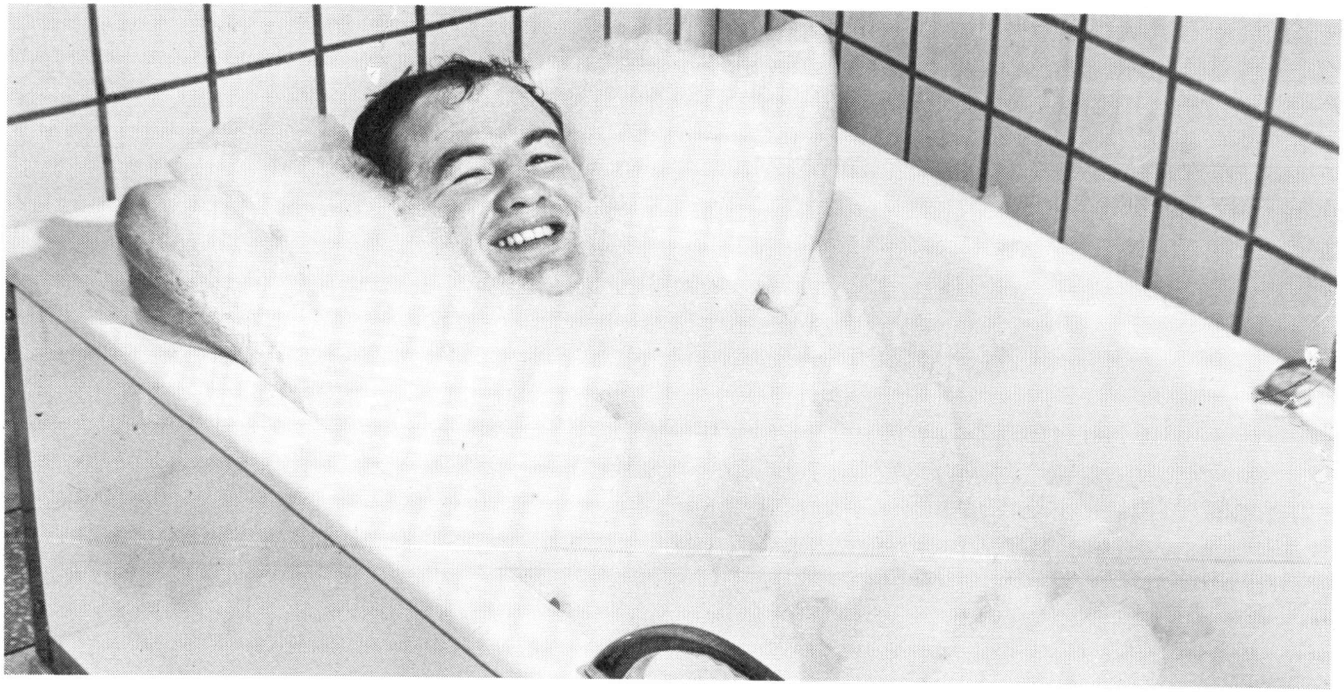

Freddie Gilroy, seen above demonstrating a more relaxing side of the fight game in a foam bath, was one of a long line of boxers from Belfast to win British, European or world titles. The press report and smaller photograph recall the more characteristic Gilroy who, in 1961, defeated his fellow Belfastman, John Caldwell, then world bantamweight champion.

BOXING

THE RING

THOMAS STREET (off Gt. George's Street), BELFAST.

WEDNESDAY NIGHT, 4th JANUARY,

At 8 o'clock. Doors Open at 7-15.

Promoter—Mr. N. JOSEPH, B.B.B.C.

SENSATIONAL TEN 3-MINUTE ROUNDS BANTAM-WEIGHT CONTEST.

JIM O'NEILL v. JOE CROFT
(CAMBUSLANG) (BOLTON).

Eight Rounds Middle-weight Contest:

TOMMY CONNOLLY v. TOM LARKIN
(BELFAST) (SHEFFIELD).

Eight Rounds Light-Weight Contest:

JACK STRATTON v. BILLY CORBETT
(Belfast) (Glasgow).

Eight Rounds Bantam-weight Contest:

DAVIE NELSON v BOBBIE TRAYNOR
(BELFAST) (DUBLIN)

M.C.—Mr. Jack Hinds, B.B.B.C.
Referee—Mr. Myers (Manchester), B.B.B.C.
Matchmaker—Mr. H. Hanley, B.B.B.C.
PRICES—1/3, 1/10; Reserved Ringside, 2/4, 3/6
Tickets now on Sale at GARDINER'S, 24 Royal Avenue.

If he had lived another day his wife would have been a year dead

A WONDERING correspondent makes his contribution to the mysteries of Ulster speech by asking why the word "roughness" should be used to mean "in good supply." He quotes the phrase: "There's always a good roughness of food about the place," when refeernce is made to a house where hospitality is assured.

From North Antrim comes a phrase which would certainly cause some bewilderment if heard elsewhere: "He didn't even say collie would ye pree." This, apparently, is another way of indicating that he was so inhospitable that he wouldn't even invite you to taste his food.

Another correspondent comments that a friend of his frequently complains that 99 times out of 100 the BBC pronounciation of secretary is "sekerty." Yet, he adds, the same grumbler thinks nothing of the Ulster form which results in the word being pronounced "seeqeterry."

It is an East Belfast correspondent who wonders what has happened to a figure who used to strike terror into the hearts of young wrongdoers in the days when kicking football in the streets with nothing more harmful than a "hankie ball" was consdiered a crime. The cry guaranteed to stop the game was "Lift it. There's a big D coming."

Would the youngster of to-day know what was meant?

Here are this week's winning letters. Those starred qualify for Pepper pounds.

✱ critic

A HOLIDAY once spent in Portstewart was made hilarious by the presence in our hotel of a very large and opinionated lady, who believed in making her presence felt.

A friend was showing off a new hat, which was really quite nice, when the large lady declared: "Don't take it ill on me when I tell ye it luks like a bucket of hen's mate."

I was taken to task for my swim suit. "You're aye big in the butt and its aye bin bought before ye were right grew."

In the evenings she became ve[illegible]ified and made a point of never using the word comment. It was always

com-ment. The most outrageous opinions were prefaced with "Well, I wud take it on meself to com-ment."

One sufferer was goaded into saying: "You'd insult the back teeth in a bullock." To this she replied: "Barge on, there. It doesn't take a feather out of me."—

A B.. Belfast.

✱ age

SOME years ago, over pint, a provincial undertaker told me of some of the unusual turns of phrase he had encountered. Some of them I have never forgotten:

"He was old for all the age he was."

"The flesh just walked off him latterly."

"If he had lived another day his wife would have been a year dead."

"He was no bother except that he tired easily when he slept."

"Will you be needin' his sasies and gallasses" (Suspenders and braces).

Retired, Co. Fermanagh.

religious

I REMEMBER a husband who described his wife as a very religious cook—it was either a sacrifice or a burnt offering.

A youth was telling a friend about a new girl with whom he had been out with and was asked "What's she like?" He replied, "Everything. Filet Mignon, potatoes, lobster, salad, ice cream everything."

It was an Ulster bride who said to her husband, "Guess what I'd made for tea, darling?" and was told. "Just serve it and I'll do my best."

J. McK.. Dundonald.

harrished

THESE are phrases never heard other than in Ulster accent:

'The children have me harrished to death." (Harrassed).

"I'm awful bad at swallying pills. I can't swally them at all."

'I'm bothered with the oul rheumy in my hinch bone."

She's got one of them Amersham heaters."

"My clappers are killing me."

"We always manage a bit of kitchen for the tea." Mrs. Anne K. Adams, Golden View Park, Carrickfergus.

more

More examples next week of the weird ways of Ulster people when they have somethin gto say. If you have your own favourite send them to John Pepper, Belfast Telegraph, Belfast BT1, 1EB, to arrive by Wednesday next, August 22.

A typical John Pepper Column. It is a regular Saturday feature in the Belfast Telegraph. Each week it rounds up and discusses letters received from Ulster people the world over, writing about the oddities and characteristics of their way of speaking.